Frederick Ross

Bygone London

Frederick Ross

Bygone London

ISBN/EAN: 9783743311114

Manufactured in Europe, USA, Canada, Australia, Japa

Cover: Foto ©ninafisch / pixelio.de

Manufactured and distributed by brebook publishing software (www.brebook.com)

Frederick Ross

Bygone London

BYGONE LONDON.

BY

FREDERICK ROSS, F.R.H.S.,

AUTHOR OF

"LEGENDARY YORKSHIRE," "YORKSHIRE FAMILY ROMANCE," ETC., ETC.

LONDON:
HUTCHINSON & CO., PATERNOSTER SQUARE.

1892.

Preface.

NOTWITHSTANDING the multitude of books that have been written relating to its history and antiquities, the History of London still remains to be written, a work that cannot, from its ocean-like infinitude of matter, be accomplished by a single hand, but will require the combined action of a multiplicity of labourers.

By London is here meant, not the vast aggregation of buildings and population spreading into four or five counties but that small fraction lying north and south of the Thames, which is under the jurisdiction of the Lord Mayor of London—that portion which was a considerable emporium of trade under the Celtic Trinobantes; a military post and seat of commerce under the Romans, with roads, of which one still retains its

PREFACE.

name of Watling Street, in the centre of London, all radiating from a central miliarium, which may still be seen, a venerable relic of sixteen centuries of age, in the wall of St. Swithin's Church; which was a capital city and place of great mercantile importance under the Saxons and the Danes, and has in the subsequent thousand years, gradually expanded its limits, and gathered population, wealth, and commerce, until it has become the capital of the world, in magnitude and wealth unprecedented, to which the capitals of other nations are but as provincial cities : so vast and rich that Blucher might well exclaim, when shewn its banks and docks, its warehouses and shops—" Ye gods! what a place to sack."

Notwithstanding the many books in existence, descriptive of the various phases of London, it appeared to the publishers there was still room for a small, handy, and compact volume, of moderate price, which should give a clear and comprehensive view of some of the more salient features of the bygone history of the old city, which they presume to hope may be found in this volume.

Contents.

	PAGE
THE WALLS AND GATES	1
EPISODES IN THE ANNALS OF CHEAPSIDE	34
BISHOPSGATE STREET WITHIN AND WITHOUT	76
ALDERSGATE STREET AND ST. MARTIN'S-LE-GRAND	118
OLD BROAD STREET	142
CHAUCER AND THE TABARD	165
THE PRIORY OF THE HOLY TRINITY, ALDGATE	178
CONVENT OF THE SISTERS MINORESSES OF THE ORDER OF ST. CLARE, ALDGATE	197
THE ABBEY OF ST. MARY OF GRACES, OR EAST MINSTER	208
THE BARONS FITZWALTER OF BAYNARD'S CASTLE	219
SIR NICHOLAS BREMBER, KNIGHT, LORD MAYOR OF LONDON	239
AN OLDEN TIME BISHOP OF LONDON: ROBERT DE BRAYBROOKE	249
A BRAVE OLD LONDON BISHOP: FULCO BASSET	262
AN OLD LONDON DIARIST	269
INDEX	291

BYGONE LONDON.

The Walls and Gates.

IN prehistoric ages the valley of the Thames formed the bed of an estuary or arm of the sea, whose waters flowed over the low lands of Essex, and whose waves dashed against the sloping uplands of Middlesex and Surrey, on whose summits now stand the Crystal and Alexandra Palaces. In process of time, by the deposition of silt brought down from the west, and of sand brought up by the flow of the tide, the estuary was reduced to a river, afterwards still further reduced in width by the embankments made by the Romans along the coast of Essex; and the land intervening between the then and the former shores became a succession of fens and morasses, some of which remained to comparatively modern times, and have their localities indicated by such names as Moorfields, Fenchurch, Marsh-gate, Lambeth, etc.

Amongst these morasses were oases of high and firm land; and beyond, spreading up and over the slopes of the uplands, there grew a dense forest, the home of wolves, boars, and other wild animals. Upon one of these spots of dry land, at the time of the invasion of Cæsar, might be seen a village of wattled or mud-built and thatched huts, inhabited by the Celtic aborigines, with cattle and hogs feeding in the midst, a few patches of cultivated land, and beyond, the forest. This was the nucleus of the mighty London of the present, and is supposed to have occupied a space of some quarter of a mile along the river shore, with Dowgate for its centre, and stretching northward as far as Cheapside. In all probability it would be surrounded by earthworks, ditches, and stockades, for the purpose of defence, and would otherwise be protected by the broad stream of the Thames, and by the Fleet river on the west, and Walbrook on the east.

When the Romans completed the subjugation of the southern part of Britain and began to make settlements, their practical sagacity at once perceived the eligibility of this spot as a centre of commerce; and in a short time it put on the appearance of a Roman city, and gradually became adorned with residential houses after the Roman fashion—whose tesselated pavements and other decorations are still often exhumed—with marts of commerce, temples of the gods, basilicæ, baths, amphitheatres, and other architectural appliances of an important city.

At what period the Romans substituted a wall of defence in place of the old earthworks is uncertain, but previous to its construction they appeared to have erected two forts on the north bank of the Thames—one at the eastern extremity of the City, where the tower now stands; the other at the western end, where the Fleet fell into the Thames. That it was an open town, or very imperfectly defended, in the middle of the first century, is evidenced by the facility with which Queen Boadicea, *temp.* Nero, entered it with her army, slaughtered the inhabitants, and most probably burnt it, as the charred remains of a great conflagration have been frequently found in making deep excavations. Henry of Huntingdon, and some other of the old chroniclers, tell us that it was first walled by Constantine the Great, at the request of his mother Helena, and that the materials he made use of were hewn stone and British bricks, and that it was in compass about three miles. Camden seems to credit this statement, from the fact that coins of the Empress Helena have been found under the wall, but as these might have been in circulation long after her death, it only goes to prove that the wall was not built before her era. Constantine died in the year 337, and we find some twenty-five years afterwards London was entered and pillaged, and the inhabitants reduced to a state of great misery, by a combined army of Picts, Scots, Saxons, and Franks, which would scarcely have been possible if it had been walled, and defended by the disciplined soldiers of the empire. The probability seems to be that the walls were either built or commenced by Theodosius, the Roman general, afterwards emperor, who in the reign of Valentinian, came to Britain with an army, utterly routed the pirates and freebooters, and entered London in triumph, where he remained for a considerable period; and we are told by Ammianus Marcellinus that before he left the island he restored to their ancient sound condition both the towns and military strongholds throughout the country, and put everything in such a state of defence that peace was maintained until the reign of Honorius, when Britain was abandoned by the Romans. Hence we may arrive at an approximate date for the building of the walls. Constantine came to the throne in 306, and Valentinian died 375: and it is almost certain that it took place some time within these 70 years, the balance of evidence seeming to refer it further to the period of the sojourn of Theodosius in Britain, or about 368-70.

Fitzstephen is the earliest writer who mentions the wall. He lived in the reign of Henry II., towards the end of the twelfth century, and describes the wall as high and thick, with seven double gates and many towers and turrets placed at proper distances. Originally there were only four exits from the City—by way of Aldgate on the east, Cripplegate on the north, Newgate on the west, and Dowgate on the south; the latter was the entrance to the "Trajectus," or ferry across the Thames, and derived its name from Dwr or Dour—water; or perhaps from Dwyr Dover, as leading to the Dover-road. Near to this gate was placed the *Miliarium*, a portion of which may still be seen in the wall of St. Swithin's Church, whence distances were measured along the roads, and from which radiated four roads—one by Dowgate and across into Kent, and three others which passed respectively through Aldgate, Cripplegate, and Ludgate. The wall commenced at the eastern fort, and had a postern gate at its commencement which occupied the position of the row of posts in Postern-row, north of the Tower, whence it ran northward to Aldgate, the eastern exit (some portions of the old wall are still remaining at the back of the houses in America Crescent); from Aldgate it went in a north-western direction between Hounds-ditch and Camomile Street to Bishopgate, whence it proceeded directly west to Cripplegate. In the street called London-wall a fragment may be seen, and the remains of a bastion may be found between St. Giles's Church and the Barber Surgeons' Hall. From this point it turned southward for a short distance down Noble Street, and again deflected to the west, arriving at Aldersgate, after which it passed St. Botolph's Church and Christ's Hospital, then turned southward at a sharp angle, coming to Ludgate (which stood immediately to the west of St. Martin's Church), and hence to the Thames. In 1276 that portion south of Ludgate was taken down, and a new wall built from Ludgate to the

Fleet river, and hence south to the Thames, so as to enclose the new Blackfriars' Monastery. It has been doubted whether the wall was continued along the river bank, but Fitzstephen says:— "London once had its walls and towers on the south, but that vast river, the Thames, which abounds with fish, and enjoys the benefit of tides, and washes the City on this side, hath in a long track of time totally subverted and carried them away;" and adds, that in his day some relics might be seen. Salmon, in his *Survey of England*, vol. i., disputes this, chiefly on the ground that we have no historical account of any great inundation such as would be necessary to effect such a result; and Maitland combats his arguments at great length, contending that a period of 777 years was quite sufficient to account for their decay and disappearance; and Lord Lyttelton remarks that long previously it had not been necessary to repair the south wall, the Tower and the bridge being amply sufficient to prevent a hostile fleet approaching the City.

In the year 1707 considerable portions of the wall were laid bare in digging for the foundations of some houses near Bishopsgate, which Dr. Woodward carefully examined, and gave a description of the materials and construction in "Remarks upon the Ancient and Present State of London: Occasioned by some Roman urns, etc., discovered near Bishopgate," originally published in the eighth volume of Leland's *Itinerary*, and afterwards separately. He says: "It was compiled alternately of layers of broad flat bricks and of ragstone." The bricks lay in double ranges, and each brick being but one inch and three tenths in thickness, the whole layer, with the mortar interposed, exceeded not three inches. The layers of stone were not quite two feet thick of our measure. To this height (eight feet) the workmanship was after the Roman manner, and these were the remains of the ancient wall. In this it was very observable that the mortar was, as usual in the Roman work, so very firm and hard that the stone itself was easily broke and gave way as that. It was thus far from the foundation nine feet in thickness. The broad thin bricks above mentioned were all of Roman make, and of the sort, as we learn from Pliny, that were in common use among the Romans, being in length one foot and a half of their standard, and in breadth one foot. The old wall having been demolished, was afterwards repaired and carried up of the same thickness to eight or nine feet in height; or, if higher, there was no more of that work now standing. All this was apparently additional, and of a make later than the part underneath it. The outside, towards the suburbs, was faced with a coarse sort of stone, not compiled with care, nor disposed into a regular method; but on the inside there appeared more marks of workmanship and art. There was not one of the broad thin Roman bricks mentioned above in all this part, nor was the mortar near so hard as in that below; but from the description it may be easily collected that this part, when first made and entire, with so various and orderly a disposition of the materials—flint, stone, and bricks—could not but carry a very elegant and handsome aspect. Upon the additional work now described was raised a wall wholly of brick, only that it terminated in battlements topped with copings of stone. It was two feet four inches in thickness, and somewhat above eight feet in height. . . . This wall was strengthened and embellished with stately towers, which on the south, together with the wall, are long since become a prey to the tide and weather; but the remains of those on the land side, being fifteen in number, are still to be seen : one thereof, about the middle of Houndsditch, is a Roman construction, composed of stone with layers of bricks. It is situated almost opposite the end of Gravel Lane, on the west of Houndsditch, and is still three stories high, but sorely decayed and rent from top to bottom in divers parts."

The height of the Roman wall is supposed to have been about twenty-two feet, and that of the towers about forty. Besides these towers there were bastions and other defensive works usual in fortifications. In Vineyard Street, on the south of Aldgate, the base of a tower about eight feet high was made use of for a new superstructure early in the last century, upon which had been fixed a stone with this inscription :—

" Glory be to God on high, who was graciously pleased in a wonderful manner to preserve the lives of all the people in this house, twelve in number, when the ould wall of this Bulwark fell down three stories high, and so broad as two cartes might enter a breast, and yet without any harm to their persones. The Lord sanctify this his great providence unto them. Amen and Amen. It was Tuesday, the 23rd September, 1651."

There is reason for believing that the first western wall ran southward, with a slight inclination to the west, from Cripplegate to the Thames, passing eastward of St. Paul's, as urns and other sepulchral remains have been found between this line and that indicated above. The Romans never buried their dead within the walls, consequently this locality must at some period have been extramural; and it would appear that as these remains have been found beneath pavements, as the City grew in population and required more space for the habitations of the living, the old graveyards were built over. Some forty years ago, in sinking a shaft in Paternoster Row, the excavators met, at a depth of eighteen feet, a stone wall of such intense hardness that it took the workmen three or four days to cut through it. This is supposed to have been a portion of the primitive wall, and is described by C. Roach Smith in the *Archæologist*, vol. xxvii., pp. 140-53.

After the departure of the Romans, the wall appears to have fallen to decay, and the City was easily taken by the Saxon pirates, who also neglected defences of this description to a great extent, trusting more to their own valour than in bricks and mortar. It would no doubt suffer greatly in the destruction of its towers and bastions in the three great conflagrations which occurred in the years 764, 798, and 801, and consumed the greater part of the City. Such being the case, it fell an easy prey to the Danes, who in 851 sailed up the Thames with a fleet of 350 ships, speedily reduced it, and garrisoned it as a basis whence to attack Wessex. Alfred the Great succeeded to the throne of Wessex in 871, and from that period to 878 he fought no less than fifty-six battles with the invaders. In 884 he laid siege to London, drove out the Danes and compelled them to capitulate, after which he repaired the walls and forts, and appointed his son-in-law, Ethered, governor. The repairs appear to have been of a substantial character, as when Anlaf and Swegen, or Sweyn, the kings of Norway and Denmark, attacked the City, with a fleet of 94 ships, in 994, the citizens were enabled to defy all their endeavours to enter within the walls, and compelled them to raise the siege with great loss, as happened again in 1013, when the city was defended by Ethelred II. But after some successes elsewhere, Sweyn returned, and again laid siege to the City; and again the citizens might have closed their gates against him, but Ethelred, their king, pusillanimously fled to Normandy, and the citizens deemed it best to submit, whereupon the gates were thrown open, the Danes admitted, and Sweyn proclaimed King of England.

Sweyn did not long enjoy this dignity; he died the following spring, when the Londoners recalled Ethelred: and he also dying soon after, Edmund Ironsides, his son, was proclaimed king, and crowned in London. Canute, the son of Sweyn, however, claimed the crown won by the prowess of his father, and came with a large fleet up the Thames, but could not pass beyond the bridge, and finding he could make no impression on the eastern walls and forts, he cut a canal across Southwark and Lambeth, availing himself of certain watercourses, and conveyed his ships into the Thames somewhere about Vauxhall, whence he sailed downward, and attacked the western walls and towers; but the undaunted bravery of the citizens and the strength of their defences compelled him to raise the siege. Soon after, however, a treaty was entered into between Edmund and Canute for the division of the kingdom: and London falling to the share of the latter, he took up his winter quarters there. By the death of Edmund a few months after, Canute became sole monarch of England.

After the battle of Hastings, William the Conqueror marched upon London, but was opposed by a body of the citizens in Southwark, whom he repulsed; but recognising their valour and perceiving the strength of the City's fortifications, he went to subdue the Western Counties, and his success in that direction showed the Londoners that the wisest and most politic course would be to submit; when the Norman duke entered the City, and was presented with the keys and acknowledged as King of England. He was no sooner in possession of the City than he caused three castles to be erected, ostensibly for the protection of the City, but really to overawe the inhabitants. These were the Tower at the eastern, and Baynard and Montfichet Castles at the western, extremity of the walls. The Tower became the residence of the Norman kings, and Baynard Castle that of the chatelain and standard-bearer of the City—offices held first by the Baynards, and afterwards by the Barons Fitzwalter. Montfichet Castle was destroyed by fire in the reign of William, and the Black Friars'

Monastery built on the site—the best of the stones being used in the re-edification of St. Paul's Cathedral, which had been destroyed by fire.

Fitzstephen speaks of the walls being "both high and thick, with seven double gates," which appear then to have been in good condition, although the south wall had been "subverted and carried away by the tide." But very soon after some portions seem to have fallen into a ruinous condition; as Roger of Wendover and Matthew Paris tell us that the barons, when in arms against King John, in 1215, entered the City by Ealdgate, and demolished the houses of the Jews, to obtain materials wherewith to repair that gate and the adjoining walls. In 1257, also, it is stated, Henry III. "caused the walls, which were greatly decayed, and destitute of towers and turrets, to be repaired in a handsomer manner than before, at the common charge of the City."

King Edward I. granted permission to Kilwarby, Archbishop of Canterbury, to take down the wall, from Ludgate to the Thames, for the purpose of enlarging the Church of the Black Friars, and in 1282 granted a murage charter to the Corporation for levying certain tolls throughout the kingdom, for making a new wall from Ludgate—westward to Fleet Bridge, along behind the houses and by the water of the Fleet to the Thames, "from the aforesaid day to the end of three years next following," from which none were exempt, saving the city of Winchester, and a few other cities, which, by composition, were to pay no Portage, Murage, or Pannage. After an enumeration of the articles to be subjected to toll, amongst which are: "Riges, Cetewal, Kanel, Frankincense, Cummin, Liquorish, Zuber, Cyromontani, Frails of Figs," etc., is added, "Whereas we have granted you for aid of the work of the walls of our City and the closure of the same, *divers customs of vendible things, coming to the said City, to be taken for a certain time, we command you that you cause to be finished the wall of the said City now begun near the Friars-preachers, and a certain good and comely tower at the head of the said wall within the water of the Thames," etc. Similar letters were issued by Edward II. in the first, second, sixth, eighth, and twelfth years of his reign; but as it was found that levying a toll on retail commodities caused an insufficient supply, the patent ran in the latter year, that—" Victualia non adducuntur, in detrimentum civitatis;" but that impositions should be levied in bulk on all merchandise brought by land or water. Richard II., in a letter to the Corporation, said in the preamble: " Know ye, that whereas the walls and forts of the City be old and weak, and for want of repair are fallen down in some places, as also the ditches of the said City are exceeding filled with dirt, dunghills, and other filth, not only to the evident danger of the said City and inhabitants thereof, but also to the manifest disgrace and scandal of the whole City," etc.; and granted to the Mayor and Corporation power to levy tolls for ten years for the purpose of placing the wall in a state of thorough repair. In order to enforce these murage tolls it was customary to have chains fixed across the entrances to the City, and no country people with provisions for sale were allowed to pass until they had paid the dues.

In the reign of Edward IV., Ralph Joscelyne, the mayor, repaired the wall from Aldgate to Aldersgate, for which purpose he caused bricks to be made in Moorfields, where also the lime brought from Kent was burnt for that purpose. This was in the year 1477, and several of the City companies—the Drapers (of which company the mayor was a member), the Skinners, the Goldsmiths, and others—contributed to the work, and placed their arms on the portions they executed. The executors of Sir John Crosby also contributed freely out of the funds they held in trust towards the same object. By an order of the Common Council each parishioner also was directed to pay sixpence every Sunday at his Parish Church until the work was completed. After this the walls were neglected and suffered to fall in ruin. Camden, writing in 1607, says that the north wall " having been repaired by one Joscelin, who was mayor, it put on, as it were, a new face and freshness, but that towards the east and west, though the barons repaired it in their wars of the demolished houses of the Jews, is all ruinous and going to decay. For the Londoners, like the Lacedæmonians of old, do slight fenced cities, as fit for nothing but women to live in, and look upon their own City to be safe, not by the assistance of stones, but by the courage of its inhabitants." Nevertheless when the Civil Wars between Charles I. and his Parliament had fairly commenced, the citizens bethought them of their walls and forts as no contemptible means of defence. London had declared most decisively for the Parliament; and in 1643, the Common Council gave directions that the ditches should be cleaned out of the accumulations of rubbish, all outside buildings cleared away, the bulwarks put in repair and mounted with cannon, and new works added to the weaker parts of the walls. The Parliament confirmed this resolution. and extended a plan of fortification, so as to include Southwark and Westminster. A chain of forts surrounding the whole, and lines of communication. were ordered to be erected. All the entrances to the City were closed excepting those at Charing Cross, St. Giles-in-the-Fields, St. John's Street, Shoreditch, and Whitechapel; and these were fortified with musket proof breastworks. To carry out these extensive works a levy was made of eight-fifteenths on all the wards of the City, which was cheerfully assented to by the citizens. and the works were commenced without delay, and carried on with such zeal and alacrity that the whole was completed in an incredibly short space of time. In the year 1647, when the dispute was raging between the Presbyterians and the Independents, the city was divided in opinion : but when the army under Fairfax advanced from Hounslow upon London, the Mayor and Corporation met and saluted the general at Charing Cross; and by an ordnance of Parliament he was constituted Constable of the Tower, the army thus becoming masters of the City. The Parliament then demanded a loan of £50,000 from the City, which was not complied with and in consequence an Act was passed for demolishing the fortifications of London, Westminster, and Southwark.

Whether the Roman wall was protected by a ditch does not appear; probably not, as the first mention we have of one being made is by Dunthorn, who informs us that William, Bishop of Ely, Regent of England when Richard I. was absent in Palestine, made a ditch round the Tower as a defence against John, the King's brother, soon after which the citizens dug a ditch round the walls generally, which they commenced about 1190, but left it unfinished until 1213, as the register of Barmondsey states, when it was recommenced, and completed in two years. This ditch was 200 feet broad, but was afterwards neglected, and gardens planted and houses built upon it. In 1354, Edward III. caused it to be cleansed; and again in 1379, by direction of Lord Mayor Philpot, as also by Lord Mayor

Fawconer, in 1414, and Lord Mayor Joceline, in 1477. In 1519, 10th Henry VIII., it was "cleansed and scowered" between Aldgate and the Tower—the chief ditcher being paid 7d. per day, the second ditcher 6d., other ditchers 5d., and every "vagabond" (labourer) one penny and meat and drink at the charge of the City. It was cleansed out again in 1549 at the expense of the trade guilds, and twenty years after, *temp.* Elizabeth, at a cost of £814 15s. 8d., at which time "it had therein great store of good fish of divers sorts." After this the expense was defrayed by letting the banks and "the whole spoil of the ditch," excepting in 1595, when the Common Council granted two-fifteens for the purpose. In the following century the ditch was filled up, excepting Fleet Ditch on the west, which, after the Fire of 1666, was, by direction of the Mayor and Court of Aldermen, ordered to be cleansed, enlarged, and made navigable for barges up to Holborn-bridge. The sides were built of freestone, and it was arranged that its banks should be lined with warehouses and wharves, but this part of the project was not carried out in its integrity. "This ditch was built and made by Sir Thomas Fitch, bricklayer, who contracted with the City for a very considerable sum, and enriched himself thereby." In 1723 the Corporation obtained an Act of Parliament for filling up the channel from Fleet-bridge to Holborn-bridge, which had become choked with mud and was no longer navigable, and to build thereon a new market in place of Stocks Market, near the Exchange, which it was proposed to dismarket and demolish, and erect on the site a Mansion House for the Lord Mayor.

We have seen that in the old Roman walls there were four gates, the exits of four roads radiating from the "milliarum," now called London Stone. These gates were—Aldgate on the east, Aldersgate on the north, Ludgate on the west, and Dowgate on the south. What were the architectural features of these gates we know not, but undoubtedly they were similar to the usual Roman gateways, with round-arched openings and fortified upper chambers for the purpose of defence.

ALDGATE, or Ealdgate, so called by the Saxons on account of its antiquity, was placed by King Eadger in the hands of the knights of the Knighten Guild, who held the soke, now called Potsoken Ward Without, by charter. Afterwards it became part of the demesne of Maud, queen of Henry I., who bestowed it upon the prior and canons of her foundation, the Priory of the Holy Trinity, along with the soke and franchise of the ward. In 1215, the barons, in their war with King John, being favoured by the Londoners, entered the City by Aldgate, which was in a ruinous condition, and repaired, or rather rebuilt it, in the Norman style, with an arched opening built from the ruins of the Jews' houses, and bulwarks of Caen stone. In the 11th Edward IV., the Bastard of Fauconbridge sailed up the Thames with his fleet, he being the admiral, to attack London in the then hopeless interest of the Lancastrian ex-king, when the Londoners hastily fortified the river front, and he landed in Essex, marched to Aldgate, and forced an entrance; but the portcullis having been lowered, separated his forces, and they were defeated and driven back to Mile-end, many being slain and others dispersed. Having fallen to decay, the gate was taken down in 1606, and rebuilt, the finishing stone having been laid in 1609. It consisted of two three-storied square flanking towers, with a deep recessed centre, containing the archway and a room above, and a footway postern in one of the towers. It was ornamented with two stone medallions, copies of two Roman coins found on digging the foundations, a figure of King James I., in gilt armour, over the arch, figures of two soldiers on the battlements, and a representation of Fortune standing on a globe. The rooms over the gate were appropriated to the Lord Mayor's carver as a residence.

ALDERSGATE, like Aldgate, was denominated Eldergate by the Saxons on account of its antiquity. It was at divers times enlarged, with additional buildings, and was rebuilt in 1617 by direction of the Corporation, William Parker, merchant tailor, contributing £1,000 towards that object. It was built with a recessed centre, and square flanking towers four stories in height. Over the arch was an equestrian figure of King James I., who entered London by this gate when he came from Scotland to succeed Elizabeth on the throne of England, and on the opposite or southern front were statues of the prophets Jeremiah and Samuel, and another representation of King James, seated in a chair of State, in his royal robes. The rooms over the postern were occupied by the Common Crier of the City.

This gate suffered great damage in the Fire of 1666, but was restored at the charge of the City, during the mayoralty of Sir Samuel Stirling.

LUDGATE, Geoffry of Monmouth informs us, was built by King Lud, *circa* A.D. 66. It was repaired and partly reconstructed by the barons, in 1215, out of the materials of the Jews' houses, and was again rebuilt in 1586, when a stone was found in the old structure bearing an inscription in Hebrew characters, "This is the station of Rabbi Moses, the son of the honourable Rabbi Isaac." During some repairs in 1260, statues of Lud, and other ancient kings, were placed upon the gate; "but," as Stow says, "these had their heads smitten off in the reign of Edward the Sixth, by unadvised persons and such who judged every image to be an idol. In the reign of Queen Mary, they were again repaired, and had new heads set to their old bodies." In 1586, being much decayed, it was entirely rebuilt by the Corporation, at a cost of £1,500, with statues of Lud and other kings on the east, and of Queen Elizabeth on the west. From the year 1378, this gate was used as a prison for freemen of the City guilty of the crimes of "debt, trespasser, accompts and contempts." It was consumed in the Fire of 1666, but substantially rebuilt, like an ordinary house, with central archway and side portions, and ornamented with statues of Queen Elizabeth, King Lud, etc.

The fourth ancient gate was the exit to the ferry across the Thames, called DOWGATE, Downgate, or Dourgate, the great road to the Kentish sea-coast, running from the opposite bank. It seems to have disappeared, along with the ferry, when the bridge was built and the gateway transferred to that locality.

By the time of Henry II. the exigencies of commerce, and, as Maitland says, "the accommodation of the citizens in repairing to their gardens and fields," necessitated more exits through the walls; and thus we find, as Fitzstephen informs us, there were then seven double gates. These Maitland conjectures to have been Aldgate, Aldersgate, Cripplegate, Ludgate, Newgate, and the Tower Postern, but it seems more probable that instead of the last-mentioned, the seventh was Bridgegate which took the place of Dowgate.

BISHOPGATE was built by some bishop of London; Strype supposes Erkenwald, *circa* 675, but Maitland thinks it was William the Norman in the reign of the Conqueror. There were effigies of two bishops on the gate, conjectured to have been Erkenwald and William, and the presumption is that the former was the original builder, and the latter the rebuilder; as, if Erkenwald were the founder, the old gate would be 400 years old in the time of William. In the reign of Henry III. it was placed under the charge of the Hanseatic Merchants of the Guildhalle Teutonicorum, who undertook to keep it in repair in consideration of certain privileges and immunities, but they neglected their duty, for which they were called to account in the reign of Edward I., upon which they paid 210 marks sterling to the Corporation for present repairs, and entered into a covenant to be less remiss in the future, and in the reign of Edward IV. they rebuilt it. In 1561 they had again made arrangements to rebuild it, but before the reconstruction was commenced they were deprived of their liberties, and the old gate remained until 1731, when it was taken down. It was a building of castellated character, with a pointed archway in the centre, and posterns in the two side towers, with statues over the central arch, and, high up in the towers, in niches.

CRIPPLEGATE dates from the Saxon era, and obtained its name from the circumstance that cripples there congregated to supplicate for alms. Maitland considers that it, and not Aldersgate, was one of the four original Roman gates. It is related that, in the year 1010, during an incursion of the Danes into East Anglia, the monks of Bury fled to London, carrying with them the sacred relics of St. Edmund, and entering by this gate, all the cripples crouching about it were miraculously healed. It was sometime a City prison for debtors and persons guilty of trespass, and was the residence of the water-bailiff of the City. In 1244, it was rebuilt by the Brewers' Company, and again in 1491, Edmund Shaa, goldsmith, and mayor in 1483, having left 400 marks for that purpose. It was repaired and beautified, and the foot postern new made, at the charge of the City of London, in 1663, during the mayoralty of Sir John Robinson, knight and baronet, and alderman of the ward. In its last aspect it was a castellated structure with battlements, two octangular turrets, a recessed centre with Tudor archway, and a side postern through one of the towers.

NEWGATE.—In the reign of William I., the church of St. Paul's was burnt, when Mauritius,

Bishop of London, commenced re-edification. In doing this he considerably enlarged the plan, and encroached so much upon the main street which ran through Cheapside, from Aldgate to Ludgate, that vehicles were compelled to take circuitous routes through narrow streets with dangerous angles, north or south of the cathedral, to reach Ludgate. The inconvenience became so great, that in the reign of Henry I., or Stephen, a new exit was made through the wall facing Holborn, to which there was better access from Cheapside, and was called Newgate, in contradistinction to the old gates. Howell, in his *Londinopolis*, says that it is a mistake to suppose that it was built so recently as the reign of Henry I., that it was of much older date, and was formerly called Chamberlaingate; and Maitland inclines to the opinion that it, and not Ludgate, was one of the four Roman gates, from the circumstance that there are vestiges of a Roman road leading in this direction. For 500 years the gate was the common prison for felons of London and Middlesex. In the year 1255, one John Offrem, a prisoner, who had killed a prior, made his escape, and Henry III. was so displeased that he committed the Sheriffs to the Tower, and inflicted a fine upon the City of 3,000 marks. In 1422, the executors of Sir Richard Whittington, out of funds bequeathed for that purpose, "builded the Gate of London called Newgate," which Grafton says "before was a most ugly and loathsome prison." The east side was repaired in 1630, and the gate was entirely destroyed in the Great Fire of London; after which it was rebuilt "with greater magnificence than any of the gates of the City." The new building was a lofty structure, with battlemented roof, a recessed centre, with pointed archway, and two five-storied sexangular towers. It was ornamented on the west side with Tuscan pilasters, with niches holding statues in the inter-columniations, one of which was a figure of Liberty, with a cat crouching at her feet, emblematical of the career of Whittington; and on the east were three niches with figures of Justice, Truth, and Mercy.

MOORGATE was built in the year 1415, by Thomas Falconer, Lord Mayor. At that time the land outside the wall in this part was a marsh, or moor, whence the name. It was made for the easier access of the citizens to their gardens and the fields beyond the marsh; and a causeway, with dykes and bridges, was constructed across the moor, which was improved by Roger Acheley, Lord Mayor in 1511. Afterwards, in the year 1606, in the mayoralty of Sir Leonard Halliday, "the moor, before an unhealthful place, was turned into pleasant walks set with trees, compassed with brick walls, and made convenient by sewers under ground for the conveyence of the water, which cost the City £5,000 or thereabouts." It was afterwards, during the mayoralty of John Baker, 1733, "new gravell'd and rail'd in a very strong and handsome manner." The old gate, having fallen to decay, was pulled down in 1672, and a new one of stone erected, with a central archway, and posterns with two stories above in the Italian style.

BRIDGEGATE, which supplanted Dowgate, was constructed along with the bridge, in the ninth or tenth century, and was situated at the southern end. In 1436 it fell, along with the tower above it, and the two southernmost arches of the bridge; and in 1471 the new gate was burnt by the Bastard Fauconbridge. It was repaired at divers times, and was considerably damaged by fire in 1726, but was reinstated within two years. As it last appeared it had a central archway, above which was one story ornamented with the City arms, and had two circular side towers, with posterns for foot passengers. This gate is historically memorable from the number of heads of traitors and victims of royal jealousy which have been placed upon it *in terrorem*. Besides these there were several posterns between the main gates, and many water gates, such as Billingsgate, Wolfsgate, Botolphsgate, etc., which, however, were only used for commercial purposes, as wharfs for the purpose of landing goods from ships and barges.

In the great Fire of London, Ludgate, Newgate, and Aldersgate were destroyed, and rebuilt. In 1760-1, eight gates being no longer necessary, and proving to be obstructions to the traffic, were sold for what the materials would fetch, and pulled down; Newgate was destroyed by the Lord George Gordon rioters in 1780. Temple Bar which was built by Sir Christopher Wren, 1670-2, has been removed to make way for the improvements about the new Law Courts; it had some historical associations connected with it, having succeeded the old gate on London Bridge for the ghastly display of traitors' heads. It has been carted away, very injudiciously, to be placed in some private grounds, whilst there was one most suitable and alone proper place for it, where it would have retained its characteristic name, stood in a conspicuous position, and have become to a certain extent an ornament, and certainly an interesting memorial of the past history of London—that spot being on the Thames embankment, as the river-side entrance to the Temple Gardens.

Episodes in the Annals of Cheapside.

THERE are many famous streets in the capitals of the world—the Rue de Rivoli, Paris; the Nevski Prospekt, St. Petersburg; the High Street, Edinburgh; the Broadway, New York; the Joseph Platz, Vienna; the High Street, Oxford; and the Via Sacra of Old Rome, with many others. All these are renowned for various characteristics of picturesque beauty, architectural grandeur, or as the scenes of important events in bygone times. In an æsthetic point of view, Cheapside is inferior to many of these, although architecturally it is now rapidly improving, and in a few years will be able to show ranges of buildings equal to those of any street in the world; but of all the streets mentioned above, excepting, perhaps, those of Edinburgh and Rome, there is not one that can compare with it for its historical associations, and for the grand series of events of national and world-wide importance which it has witnessed during the thousand years of its existence. We purpose to bring before the reader a few of the more striking and picturesque of these events, which have occurred at different periods of its history, which will have a certain amount of value as serving to illustrate the modes of living, the customs and amusements, the fluctuations of opinion in politics and religion, the relations between king and people, and the ancient municipal glories of the citizens of London in bygone centuries.

Wondrously different was the Westchepen of the eleventh century when the Norman Conqueror granted his brief and pithy charter to the citizens of London, from that of the nineteenth, with its stately edifices, its asphalted pavement, and its rush and roar of never ceasing traffic. It was then somewhat like an ill-tended country road, in the summer rough and uneven and full of deep holes, and in winter a quagmire of mud and filth knee deep, with better beaten causeways at the sides for pedestrian traffic. It is recorded by Stow that in 1091, a terrible hurricane passed over London, when 600 houses were blown down, and the roof of the Church of St. Mary-le-Bow, erected a few years previously, was lifted off, carried some distance, and dashed into the street with such violence that four of the rafters, twenty-five feet in length, were driven into the earth, "the ground being of a moorish nature," leaving only four feet exposed, "which were fain to be cut even with the ground, because they could not be plucked out." The houses stood apart from each other like cottages in a village, and were thatched with straw, which was the cause of many fires, one occurring two years after the great storm, in which nearly the whole of the remaining houses were consumed; and so did the citizens continue to rebuild their habitations after each successive fire, until 1245, when it was ordained that for the future they should be covered with tiles or slates, instead of straw, in the chief streets, "especially those close together, which were but few in number, for in Cheapside was a void place called Crown Field, from the Crown Inn which stood at the end of it." This field was at the end of Soper's Lane, by Bucklersbury, and upon it were erected stages for spectators of pageants. It was sold, 2 Ed. IV., to Sir Richard Cholmley, but does not appear to have been utilized immediately for building purposes, as we hear it spoken of in the time of Henry VII.

The curfew bell was tolled from the tower of

St. Mary, and on the top lanterns were suspended and lighted at night, "whereby travellers to the City might have the better sight thereof, and not miss their ways."

For the supply of water there was a great standard or conduit at the east end, where the Poultry commences, and a smaller one opposite Old Change, by Paul's Gate, and opposite Wood Street stood one of the Eleanor Crosses, erected in 1290, which having become decayed by time, was re-edified by John Hatherley, Lord Mayor, who added to it a fountain. These conduits were the frequent scenes of punishments for misdeeds and executions. Wat Tyler beheaded Sheriff Lyon at the western standard, and there Jack Cade chopped off the head of Lord Say; there also Stapleton, Bishop of Exeter, and treasurer to Edward II., was beheaded in 1326 "by the burgesses of London." In the same localities also was the pillory erected, where Prynne, Burton, and Bastwick, had their ears lopped off, and there Defoe and a multitude of other less known defenders of public rights and freedom of conscience have been exposed, sometimes to the derision, at others to the sympathy, of the mob.

In the Plantagenet and Tudor eras Cheapside

had assumed a different and more street-like aspect. Continuous lines of houses, with gables forming a vandyke sky line, with crossed timberings and latticed windows, ran down each side, with the steeple of St. Mary-le-Bow, which had fallen in 1271, and "slain many people, men, women, and children," and been restored gradually until the finishing stone was placed in 1469, standing proudly in the centre of the southern line. At the eastern end, between Laurence Lane and a house, called the "cage," was West Chepe Market, the goods being exposed for sale on stalls, which were let at 13s. 4d. the standing, causing much bickering between the street-sellers and the shopkeepers, in front of whose doors they stood, and whose goods were often seized and burnt at the standards for deficiencies in weight, or for inferiority in quality. The Eleanor Cross, which had been rebuilt in 1441, and the eastern and the western conduits still gave forth their supplies of water. The appearance of the cross is indicated in an old print of the procession of Edward VI. to his coronation in 1547; and again, with one of the conduits, in La Serre's view of Cheapside, with the procession of Catharine de Medicis, *temp.*

Charles I. The shops were open in front like modern butchers' shops, and the goods exposed for sale on bunks. Lydgate, in his "Lackpenny" ballad, thus speaks of them :—

> "Then to the Chepe I gan me drawn,
> Where much people I saw for to stand,
> One offered me velvet, silk, and lawn,
> Another he taketh me by the hand,
> 'Here is Paris thread, the finest in the land :'
> I never was used to such things, indeed.
> And, wanting money, I could not speed."

The 'prentices of Cheapside were a conspicuous feature of the street at this period. During the day they paraded up and down in front of their masters' shop, crying "What d'ye lack: what d'ye lack?" followed by an enumeration and laudation of the articles within, and the wonderful bargains to be picked up; and in the evening listening eagerly for the sound of the curfew bell as the signal for shutting up shop. Stow tells us that in his time the bell-ringer was sometimes late, and that the 'prentices, precursors of the "Early Closing Movement" of our own time, addressed him as follows :—

> "Clerk of the Bow-bell, with the yellow locks,
> For thy late ringing thy head shall have knocks."

The bell-ringer, knowing that they would be as

good as their word, and deeming "discretion to be the better part of valour," replies :—

"Children of Chepe, hold you all still,
For you shall have Bow-bell ring at your will."

These 'prentices were a pugnacious race of mortals, and were ever ready to issue forth at the cry of "Clubs! clubs! 'Prentices! 'Prentices!" leaving the shop to take care of itself, to join in any fray that was going on in the street, especially if it were a demonstration against a foreign interloper in trade. They waited upon their master and mistress at their meals, and on Sundays and saint-days followed them demurely to church, carrying hassocks for them to kneel upon. In the summer evenings, after the shops were shut and evening prayer over, as Stow tells us, they were wont "to exercise their wasters and bucklers, and the maidens, one of them playing upon a timbrel, in sight of their masters and dames, to dance for garlands hanged across the streets," and on holidays they went out to Finsbury Fields, and other open places, and exercised themselves in leaping, dancing, shooting, wrestling, casting the stone, etc., but especially in bow and arrow practice.

Chaucer, in the *Cook's Tale*, thus describes the 'prentice of Cheapside :—

> "A prentice dwelt whilom in our citee ;
> At every bridale would he sing and hoppe ;
> He loved bet the taverne than the shoppe,
> For when ther any riding was in Chepe,
> Out of the shoppe thider wold he lepe,
> And till that he had all the sight ysein.
> And danced wel, he wold not come agen."

Some of the more salient features in the past of Cheapside which present themselves to our view in the gradual unrolling of the panorama of the ten centuries are very varied in their character. We behold a strange intermingling of gorgeous processions in honour of the birth, marriage, and coronation of royal personages, with the pillory, the stocks, and the executioner's block, and the accompanying lopping-off of hands, ears, and heads, and whippings at the cart tail ; Lord Mayors' shows, generally more grotesque than refined, and trade guild demonstrations of splendid liveries and floating banners ; combined with 'prentices' club frays, and fights between rival trade companies, which seldom ended without bloodshed ; tilting at the quintain ; tournaments and joustings ; alongside with insurrectionary risings and outbursts of religious fanaticism.

A.D. 1196. At this period the rich and the noble of the land were chiefly of the Norman race, and the poor almost all Saxons, who were ground down to the earth by the tyranny and oppression of their masters, to which they submitted with a sullen dogged obedience, having still within them that spirit of freedom which animated the breasts of their ancestors previous to the Norman Conquest. Richard Cœur de Lion was king, and had just been liberated from his captivity. He ruled the kingdom with a high hand, and had said on one occasion, when remonstrated with for raising money by unconstitutional means, "Have I not a right to do what I like with my own? I would sell London itself if I could find a purchaser." At this juncture up rose a lawyer, one William Fitzosbert, otherwise called Longbeard, who seems to have been a designing character, and desirous of currying favour with the people, he proclaimed himself the advocate of the poor, the redresser of their wrongs, and the unflinching enemy of their oppressors. He soon had a gathering around him of the penniless and discontented serfs, amounting eventually to 50,000 men, armed with bows and arrows, rudely fashioned pikes, clubs, axes, hedge stakes, and other similar weapons. This army—or rather mob—went about offering insults to the rich, breaking open their houses and plundering them in broad daylight. The Corporation had then but little authority and power, and were not able to cope with so formidable an insurrection: and Archbishop Hubert, the chief justiciary, summoned the leader to appear before him, who came, however, so numerously attended, that it was deemed wise to dismiss him with a rebuke. After this the outrages of the insurgents became more barefaced and open, as well as more numerous: whereupon more vigorous measures were taken, and after murdering an officer sent to apprehend him, Fitzosbert, with a concubine and a few followers, took refuge in the church of St. Mary-le-Bow, and fortified it against his pursuers, defying them for some time, many persons being killed in the assault, until at length a fire of damp straw was lighted beneath, the smoke of which compelled the garrison to issue forth, and after a fight in the street, they were captured and carried to the Tower, before the judges, who condemned them to death. "And then," says Stow, "he (Fitzosbert) was by the heels drawn to the Elmes in Smithfield and there hanged with nine of his fellows, where because his favourers came not to deliver him, he forsook Mary's son (as he termed Christ our Saviour), and called upon the devil to help and deliver him. Such was the end of this deceiver, a filthy fornicator, a secret murderer, a pollutor of concubines, and (amongst his other detestable acts) a false accuser of his elder brother, who had brought him up in learning, and done many things for his preferment." The people, however, looked upon him as a martyr, secured his body, carried away the broken-up gibbet and the bloodstained earth as relics, and reports were afterwards spread abroad of sundry wonderful miracles which had been worked by their sacred influence.

A.D. 1236. An aspect of a very different and much more pleasing character was that which Cheapside assumed on one occasion in this year. King Henry III. had in January married with great magnificence at Canterbury, Eleanor, second daughter of Raymond, Earl of Provence, and it was when she passed through the City, on her way to Westminster to be crowned, that a civic display was made in Cheapside, which surpassed in pomp and splendour everything which had preceded it, and which is the earliest of which we have any detailed account. The street was hung with arras, silk and cloth draperies of gay colours, and banners and pennons floating from the housetops and windows, accompanied by many strange devices, and pageants on scaffolds along the route. Andrew Bockrel, the mayor, with the sheriffs and aldermen, and a following of 360 citizens, rode forth to meet the king and queen, and escort them through the City to Westminster. They were all clad in long robes, lavishly embroidered with gold; their other garments were of silk, diversified in colour, and their horses were covered with trappings reaching to the ground, covered with embroidery and blazonry of arms. Each man carried in his hand a gold or silver cup, emblematic of the Lord Mayor's right to serve the office of chief butler at the coronation feast, and they were preceded by trumpeters. In the evening the city was illuminated with lamps, cressets, and other lights "without number," Cheapside presenting a most brilliant effect, with the bonfires blazing up from the ground, lights of different kinds gleaming from the frontages of the houses, from end to end of the street, and multitudes of men, with lighted cressets on their shoulders, marching hither and thither, and mingling with others bearing torches, a scene infinitely more picturesque than the commonplace gas illuminations of the present.

A.D. 1249. In this year King Henry III. made a raid upon the shopkeepers of Cheapside, who, true to their instinctive abhorrence of regal interference with their liberties, presented so formidable an opposition to his demands that he was fain to give way. Stow thus narrates the occurrence: " This year the King kept his Christmas at London, with the meanness of spirit worthy of himself, for he begged, as it were, large new year's gifts of the citizens. But the money on that occasion not being deemed sufficient, Henry soon after sent and imperiously demanded much greater sums. This message occasioned a great alarm amongst the citizens, who justly complained that no regard was had to honour, justice, conscience, nor religion; and that their liberties, which they had so often dearly bought, and had so many times been confirmed and sworn to, were not able to protect them from being treated as the worst of the slaves ; yet, notwithstanding these great truths, they were compelled to pay the tyrant the sum of £2,000, a very great sum at that time. Nor did these wicked proceedings stop here, for many shopkeepers in the City were spoiled of their goods (especially those for the use of the kitchen) by the order of that iniquitous prince." We may fancy the commotion that would be excited in Cheapside when the king's officers appeared and seized the goods which were displayed on the bunks for sale, and can only wonder that the valorous 'prentices did not raise their usual war cry, seize their clubs, and drive the officers back with a sound thrashing to their master who sent them. Whether they did attempt to defend their master's property in this their usual fashion is not recorded, but Stow adds : " These diabolical oppressions caused many of the most eminent citizens to retire into the country, choosing rather to cohabit with brutes than to dwell in the capital of so wicked a tyrant. . . . Henry, being at last conscious of his having frequently and unjustly imposed upon the citizens of London by many heavy and intolerable exactions, resolved to reconcile himself with them; and, in order thereunto, commanded them to attend him at Westminster, where, being assembled in the great hall, he, in the presence of his nobility, solemnly promised that for the future they should live happily under his government, and not be liable to such grievous taxations as formerly."

A.D. 1257. Sir Hugh Bigot, an itinerant judge, held a court in the City, although contrary to the ancient rights and liberties of the citizens, and made an example in Cheapside of certain bakers guilty of malpractices such as giving short weight and supplying an inferior article, "by setting them upon a tumbrell or dung-cart, wherein they were exposed in the streets as bawds usually were,"—a very wholesome punishment, which might be revived with advantage in the present day as an example to the adulterators of food.

A.D. 1262 and 1264. At the eastern end of Cheapside is a street called the Old Jewry, a name formerly applied to a limited district westward of Lothbury, and so called from being the principal Jews' quarter of the early race of Jews, who were banished the kingdom *temp.* Edward I., and where they had a synagogue. Here they lived, as well as about Jewin Street, and in a Jewery near the Tower, and then, as now, made great wealth by the practice of usury, and despoiling the Gentiles by means of hard bargains and crafty sharp practice in money dealings, which gave rise to a great deal of ill-will between the two races, much maltreatment, massacres, and unjust demands of money from the Jews, by the kings and other authorities, and the frequent pillaging of their houses by mobs.

In 1189, a general massacre of the Jews took place at the coronation of Richard I., the survivors living in constant peril of murder and confiscation, an instance of the latter occurring in 1241. when the Jews of London were fined 20,000 marks because the Jews of Norwich had circumcised a Christian child.

In 1262, a fierce quarrel broke out between a Christian and a Jew, in the Church of St. Mary Cole, in the Poultry. relative to some money transactions, which proceeded from words to blows, and the Jew, having dangerously wounded his adversary, fled into the Jewry for refuge, pursued by a mob of idlers who had witnessed the fray, and of 'prentices from the shops, nothing loth to join in a Jew-hunting frolic. The Jew was captured in his own house, dragged forth, and bludgeoned to death. Not satisfied with that, the mob fell upon the inhabitants of the quarter and murdered them indiscriminately, afterwards plundering and burning their houses.

Two years afterwards the mob was again in arms, arising out of an attempt on the part of a Jew to extort more than the legal interest (twopence per week) for £20, which he had lent to a Christian. They attacked the "Jewery" in great force, destroyed the synagogue—the first erected in England—massacred 500, or according to another authority, 700 Jews, male and female, and "spoiled the residue of their property."

In the Westminster Parliament of 1273, laws were enacted to restrain their exorbitant rates of usury, and in 1290, by an Act of the Parliament assembled at Northampton, they were banished the realm, and all their immovable property confiscated. The number who were thus driven forth amounted, according to Matthew of Westminster, to 16,160, and thus ended the first race of Jews in England, from which period until the middle of the seventeenth century, although there might be individuals, there was no organised body of Jews in the land.

A.D. 1269. In this year, the 53rd of the

reign of Henry III., a great fight took place between the Goldsmiths and the Taylors Companies, which is thus graphically described by Fabyan: "In this lili. yere in ye moneth of November fyll a very aulnce atweene the felysshyppes of Goldsmythes and Tayloures of London, whiche grewe to makynge of parties, so that with the Goldsmythes take partie the felyshep or craft of—and with the Tayloures held ye craft of Stayners; by meane of this moche people uyghtly gaderyd in the streetes in harneys, and at length as it were prouyded, the thirde nyght of the sayd parties mette upon the number of V. C. men on both sydes and ran togyder, with such vyolence, that some were slayne and many wounded. Then outcry was was made that ye shyreffes, with strengthe of other comers, came to the ryddynge of theym, and of theym toke certayne persones and sent them into dyvers prysons and upon the morrowe such serche was made, yt the moste of the chief causers of that fray were taken and put in warde Then vpon the Fryday followynge Saynt Katteryn's daye, sessyons were kepte at Newgate by the Mayre and Lawrence de Broke, iustice, and others; where xxx. of the sayd persones were arregned of felony, and xiii. of theym caste and hanged."

A.D. 1330. King Edward II. had been murdered in Berkeley Castle, and his son, Edward III., reigned in his stead, and now, five years after the decapitation of Bishop Stapleton, Cheapside was witness of a scene of a more joyous character. Unsuitable as it might be deemed nowadays, with its endless throng of cabs, omnibuses, and other vehicles, for such a display, it was then not unfrequently the chosen spot for tournaments and jousts. Two years before, the young King had married Philippa of Hainhault, and this year she had given birth to an infant, afterwards the famous Black Prince. In honour of this event, and to do honour to the visit of some French ambassadors, the King gave orders for a tournament to be held in Cheapside. The street was decorated with tapestries and silver draperies, pendant on the walls, and banners streaming from the roofs. The bright eyes of beauteous damsels glanced in the windows of the houses, and the street was filled with a crowd of gaily dressed holiday-makers. The lists were formed between Wood Street and Queen Street, and the ground bestrewn with sand to prevent the horses slipping. There was seen all the glory and paraphernalia of heraldry. Kings-at-arms and pursuivants, decked in habits emblazoned with arms, trumpeters, and other officials; prancing steeds, bestridden by knights in full panoply, with their achievements blazoned on their shields, accompanied by their esquires bearing their arms. Across the street had been erected a scaffold, shaped like a tower, whereon sat Philippa and the ladies of her court, the great centre of attraction for the spectators in the street below. Thirteen knights entered the lists on each side; stalwart men and the flower of chivalry. Their esquires handed to them their lances, and making deep obeisance to the Queen, they ranged themselves at each end for the onset, when the trumpets sounded and they dashed forward. Scarcely, however, had they done so when the scaffold on which the Queen sat came down with a terrific crash, which stopped the jousters in midway. The King rushed to the spot, anxious for the safety of the Queen, but fortunately found that no one had been hurt beyond a few bruises and a terrible fright. Great confusion prevailed, and the King, in a tempest of rage, vowed that all the careless carpenters who had constructed the stage should be put to death, but the Queen, says Stow, "took great care to save the carpenters from punishment, and through her prayers, which she made on her knees, she pacified the King and council, and thereby purchased great love of the people." After this the King caused a stone shed, called Sildham, to be built in front of Bow Church, "for himself, the Queen, and other estates to stand in, there to behold the joustings and other shows at their pleasure." It served this purpose until the year 1410, in the reign of Henry VI., when it was disposed of to Stephen Spilman, William Marchford, and John Wattel, mercers, for business purposes, with the condition that "The kings of England and other great estates, as well as those of foreign countries repairing to this realm, should be entitled to make use of it for witnessing the shows of the City, passing through Westchepe."

At the western standard by Paul's Gate, Jack Cade, the rebel leader, in 1450, caused Lord Say to be decapitated.

A.D. 1382-1445. In the interval between these dates, Cheapside was the scene of much royal pageantry of great splendour. When

Anne of Bohemia, the first Queen of Richard II., entered London after her marriage, in 1382, a castle, with towers, was erected in Cheapside, on whose battlements stood a bevy of fair maidens, who flung in their path counterfeit gold coins, and threw over them, as it were, showers of butterflies made of gold leaf; and when she and Richard passed in procession through Cheapside, afterwards, to celebrate his reconciliation with the City, after a fierce quarrel, a tower was erected, whence issued copious streams of red and white wine for all comers, the King and Queen quaffing draughts therefrom out of golden goblets, and an "angel descending from a cloud crowned them with golden circlets." In 1423 Katherine of Valois, widow of Henry V., after visiting St. Paul's Cathedral, passed through Cheapside, seated in a chair of state, with her infant king, Henry VI., in her lap, whence she proceeded to Newington Manor House. Henry VI. and his queen—the masculine and brave, but unfortunate, Margaret of Anjou—passed along Cheapside with much pageantry on the occasion of their marriage, in 1445, when they halted by the great conduit to witness a play called *The Five Wise and the Five Foolish Virgins*, who were personated with great spirit by ten City maidens. Twenty-seven years after—in 1472—the corpse of the weak and unfortunate monarch, after his suspicious death in the Tower, and the fall of the Lancaster dynasty, passed along Cheapside in mournful funereal silence, by torchlight, and with the face exposed, that all might see that the last of the Lancasters was really dead, on its progress to St. Paul's, and hence to Windsor for burial.

A.D. 1510. Perhaps the most splendid of the sights of Cheapside was the setting of the Marching Watch on the Vigil of St. John the Baptist, in June, and on that of Saints Peter and Paul in July. The City Watch was instituted in the year 1253 by Henry III., and consisted of a body of substantial citizens, with an alderman or magistrate at their head, for each ward, to protect the houses from robbery and the streets from outrages by night—crimes which had hitherto been very rife; and it was ordained that if anyone suffered loss or violence whilst the guard was on duty he should receive compensation from the ward. The Marching Watch was a grand processional display of fire and light, banners and music, glittering armour and flashing weapons, bonfires in the streets, and numberless cressets borne aloft. The citizens' wives and daughters, apparelled in their most fascinating costumes, occupied the windows; men and boys clambered on the gabled roofs; whilst in the street below tables were spread with viands and provided by the citizens, which were presided over by their 'prentices, attired in their blue gowns and yellow hosen, like the Christ's Hospital boys of our time, who invited the passers-by—more especially if they were young and pretty and of the other sex—to partake of their masters' cheer.

On the Vigil of St. John in 1510, Henry VIII., then a frolicsome young man of nineteen, who had only been a year on the throne, with a companion or two, perhaps Charles Brandon, came from Westminster, disguised as a yeomen of the guard, to see this setting of the Watch, of which he had heard so much. He came from Westminster in a public wherry, and landing at Bridewell Stairs, proceeded on foot, like a modern Haroun al Raschid, mingling with the people and cracking jests with them as he went along. He stationed himself at the cross in West Cheap, where he saw the proceedings admirably, and after partaking, most probably, of a cake and a flagon of ale at some hospitable citizen's door, he returned, so much struck with the splendour of the festival that he vowed he would bring the Queen (Catherine of Arragon, whom he had married the previous year) to see it on the next occasion, in July.

The Vigil of Saints Peter and Paul arrived, and the gay monarch, faithful to his promise, and wishing to give pleasure to his queen, dreaming not then of divorces and the headman's axe, with which he became so familiar in after life, brought her in regal state and pomp, accompanied by a crowd of nobles and court ladies, to see the civic spectacle, which they witnessed from the hall of the Mercers' Company in Cheapside The street itself, before the procession was arranged, was a sight worth seeing, and one to be remembered for many a long day. Huge bonfires were blazing up in different parts; the houses were hung with tapestry, and were lighted up with oil lamps and "branches of iron curiously wrought, containing hundreds of lamps, lighted at once, which made a great show;" timber stages, hung with variously coloured stuffs, and the latticed windows were filled with elegantly-dressed ladies, whose diamonds flashed in the light; banners and pennons floated in the evening breeze; "every man's door was shadowed with green birch, long fennel, St. John's-wort, and such like, garnished upon with beautiful flowers;" whilst prancing steeds in gay trappings, armed men with plumed casques, city and guild officials in gay liveries and a crowd of citizens, male and female, in the quaint costume of the period, mingled in picturesque groups below. After sunset the procession was arranged, and set out. First came a band of music, followed by the officials of the Corporation in parti-coloured liveries, and the sword-bearer mounted on a gaily-trapped steed, and in armour. Then came the Mayor on a magnificent horse with housings reaching to the earth, accompanied by a giant; two pages, mounted; a band of morris dancers, footmen, and three pageants. After him came the sheriffs, similarly attended with giants, morris dancers, and torchbearers, but with only two pageants. Then followed a cloud of demi-lancers, in armour, with the City arms emblazoned on their backs and breasts; a company of archers with their bows bent; pikemen and halberdiers, in corslets and helmets; and billmen, with helmets and aprons of mail.

The whole body consisted of about 2,000 men, and between the divisions were bands of drummers, fifers, and whifflers, and standard and ensign bearers. Interspersed amongst them were 940 men bearing lighted cressets—iron frames filled with pitched rope, which blazed up and sent forth volumes of black smoke, "which showed at a distance like the light of a burning city," and the same number of men to supply the cressets with fresh supplies of fuel. Two hundred of these were supplied by the City; 500 were supplied at the expense of the City companies, and the remainder were the ordinary watchmen.

The midsummer watch was kept up until 1539, when Henry VIII., considering the great expense it was to the City, caused it to be abolished. It was revived, however, in 1548, and continued until 1569, when in consequence of its bringing together "abundance of rogues, pickpockets, quarrellers, whoremongers, and drunkards," it was again abolished, and although some attempts were made afterwards to restore it, they were not successful.

A.D. 1485-1610. In the interval between these dates, Cheapside was the scene of many a grand spectacle, and it may be added of many a so-called vindication of justice in the way of barbarous mutilations and inhuman executions.

A.D. 1513. The Cheapsides 'prentices, of whom we have spoken, were a turbulent and unmanageable element of the community, keeping their clubs at hand in the shops, to be ready at any moment to rush out and join a fray, and many a broken head they gave and got in these fights, which generally arose, not so much out of malice as from pure love of contention for mastery, which then developed itself in this rough way as it now displays itself in games of cricket and athletic sports. There was one class of persons, however, against whom they had a special hatred, and nothing pleased them better than to insult them with vile speeches, drag them in the gutter or belabour them with their clubs. These were the foreign merchants, importers of silks, wine, and other commodities; the Lombard money-lenders and stranger craftsmen and citizens, who, they said, impoverished the English traders and carried away the English gold. This jealousy continued to grow, and was brought to a crisis by a Lombard seducing a citizen's wife, and obtaining through her, his plate chest, and afterwards causing the citizen to be arrested for a debt for his wife's board and lodging during the time she was at his house. A rumour got abroad that on the ensuing May Day a sort of Bartholomew's massacre should take place, and that all foreigners found in London then would be put to death. The 'prentices now began to insult and ill-treat them as they passed along the street, and several fled from the city. A report of these proceedings reached the king, and Wolsey sent for the mayor and charged him to see that the peace was kept in the city, which he assured the cardinal he was quite capable of maintaining, and departed. This was about four o'clock on the eve of May Day, and on his return to the city he assembled the magistrates and council, amongst whom was Sir Thomas More, ex-under-sheriff, when, after some discussion, it was decided to issue an order to the citizens to have their doors closed at nine o'clock, and to keep all their 'prentices and servants within until nine the following morning, and the aldermen went to their respective wards to see that this mandate, which had been confirmed by the king and council, was obeyed.

After the issuing of this order, which only

took place about half-an-hour before nine, Alderman Sir John Munday, on going down Cheapside found two young fellows playing at bucklers in the middle of the street, and a number of other young men looking on. He ordered them to desist and go within doors, and upon their asking him why, instead of explaining the order, which they had no knowledge of, he threatened to send them to the compter, and after a little altercation, seized one of the youths to commit him to prison. "But," says Stow, "the 'prentices resisted the alderman, taking the young man from him, and cried, ''Prentices! 'prentices! clubs! clubs!' Then out of every door came clubs and other weapons, so that the alderman was put to flight. Then more people arose out of every quarter, and forth came serving-men, watermen, courtiers, and others, so that by eleven o'clock there were in Cheap 600 or 700, and out of St. Paul's Churchyard came about 300. From all places they gathered together and broke open the compters, took out the prisoners committed thither for hurting the strangers. They went also to Newgate and took out Studley and Bets, committed for the like cause. The mayor and sheriffs were present and made proclamation in the king's name, but were not obeyed." After this they went in separate bands, breaking open and plundering the houses of the foreigners, until about three in the morning, when they began to disperse, and being thus disunited, the authorities were enabled to capture about 300 of the rioters and place them in prison. Sir Roger Cholmley, lieutenant of the Tower, had come forth with a military force, "and shot off certain pieces of ordnance against the City, but did no great hurt." About five o'clock the Earl of Shrewsbury and other nobles, and the prior of St. John's, Clerkenwell, came with what forces they could get together, as did the Inns of Court, "but before they came the business was over."

A special commission of oyer and terminer was issued to the Duke of Norfolk and other lords, with the Lord Mayor, aldermen, and justices, to try the prisoners. The court was held in the Guildhall, on the 2nd of May, whither the delinquents, to the number of 278 persons, were brought, tied together with ropes, and escorted by 1,300 men. On the 4th, thirteen of them were condemned to be hanged, drawn, and quartered, in divers parts of the City; which sentence was carried out with great barbarity, in the presence of Lord Edward Howard, " a knight marshal, who shewed no mercie, but extreme crueltie to the poore younglings in their execution."

A few days after, Lincolne, Shirwin, and Bets, instigators of the affray, with divers others, were dragged on hurdles to be hanged at the Standard in Cheapside. They were placed under the gallows with the ropes round their necks, when a reprieve arrived. The people shouted "God save the king," and the condemned were taken back to prison. On the 14th, the Recorder and some aldermen waited upon the king at Greenwich, to solicit pardon for the rest of the prisoners, which he bluntly refused, but ordered them to be brought before him at Westminster on the 22nd. On that day the king sat in state, attended by "the cardinal and many great lords," and the mayor and aldermen of London. "The king commanded that the prisoners should be brought forth, so that in came the poore younglings and old false knaves, bound in ropes all along, one after the other, in their shirts, and everie one a halter about his necke, to the number now of foure hundred men and eleven women. And when all were come before the king's presence,

F

the cardinall sore laide to the maior and commonaltie their negligence; and to the prisoners he declared that they had deserved death for their offence. Then the prisoners cried 'Mercie, gratious lord, mercie!' Herewith the lords altogether besought his grace of mercie, at whose sute the king pardoned them all. Then the cardinall gave unto them a good exhortation to the great gladnesse of the hearers. Now when the generall pardon was pronounced, all the prisoners shouted at once, and altogether cast up their halters into the hall roofe, so that the king might perceive they were none of the discreetest sort. Then were all the gallows within the Citie taken downe, and many a good prayer made for the king."

And thus came to an end the proceedings in connection with the frolic of the Cheapside 'prentices, on what was long afterwards called "Evil May Day."

When King John, in 1215, granted a mayor, it was stipulated that he should present himself before the king or his justices for approval, whence arose the annual procession on Lord Mayor's Day. At first it was a very simple matter, the mayor riding on horseback accompanied by the aldermen, and preceded by the beadle and a company of minstrels. It gradually, however, added new features, such as banner bearers, standards emblazoned with arms, trumpeters, " men apparelled like devils and wild men to clear the way with squibs," "savages or green men " with fireworks for the same purpose, wild animals of various kinds, emblematic figures and devices, many exceedingly quaint and grotesque, and some with punning allusions to the mayor. But the most conspicuous features of the shows of the 16th and 17th centuries were the pageants, a species of emblematical stage representation provided by the company which had the honour of giving the mayors. These pageants displayed a great deal of imagination and mechanical skill, and sometimes cost nearly a thousand pounds.

Sir John Norman is supposed to have been the first mayor who went to Westminster by water, whither he was rowed with silver oars, in 1621, for which he was lauded in verse as " The Sun in Aries," by Middleton, the Laureate.

From 1639 to 1655 the prevalence of Puritanism and the civil war together abolished the show, as did the Plague and the Fire from

1664 to 1671. In 1703 the pageants were discontinued, much to the regret of the people, who looked upon them as the best part of the show, and were especially delighted with some time-honoured representations which were repeated year by year, and never lost their interest, such as that of the Goldsmiths, in which St. Dunstan, their patron saint, seized the devil by his nose with the tongs, and made him roar with pain.

As an illustration of this olden-time mode of celebrating the inauguration of a new mayor, we have selected a pageant of the Fishmongers' Company, in the procession of Sir John Lemon, 1616, of which company he was a member. The pageant consisted of several sections: 1. The trade pageant, "A Fisshing Busse," ornamented with carvings of fish and other devices, the company's crest at the head and St. Peter's keys at the stern, with three fishermen aboard, one casting the net and the others distributing live fish among the crowd. 2. A dolphin, argent, naisant and crowned, part of the company's arms. "Arion, a famous musician and poet, rideth on backe." 3. The Emperor of Morocco, in regal costume, with crown and sceptre, "gallantly mounted on a golden leopard, and hurling gold and silver everywhere about him." He is attended by six tributary Moorish kings "carrying ingots of gold and silver and each a dart." 4. A lemon tree, in reference to the name of the Lord Mayor, with a pelican at the foot feeding her young with the blood of her own breast, emblematic of the love the chief magistrate has for the citizens. Around sit the "five senses, picturing flower, fruit, rind, pith, and juice." This portion is preceded by a winged figure, seated on a white horse, and bearing a sword, eight men in armour bearing emblazoned banners, and two trumpeters. 5. A man in armour, on a white horse, carrying the head of Wat Tyler on a spear, and five men in armour bearing truncheons. 6. A merman and mermaid, heraldically habited with gold chains, and riding on the sea waves. These are the supporters of the company's arms. 7. "The Fishmongers' Pageant Chariot," pyramidal in form, with thirteen allegorical figures, the upper part forming a throne, and seated thereon a winged and crowned figure, over which is a canopy with the Fishmongers' crest. In front of the throne sits King Richard II., in golden armour, whose life was preserved by Walworth, the winged figure above being his guardian angel, who inspired Sir William to use his dagger. There are also numerous children seated in rows above each other, splendidly dressed, representative of the Royal virtues. The stages of this part of the pageant are made to appear as if passing over the sea waves. 8. "The Fishmongers' bower." An arched recess with double columns, adorned with shields of arms of former mayors of the company. This is supposed to have been to a certain extent a copy of the tomb of Sir William Walworth, who lies thereon, dressed in a purple robe trimmed with ermine, and a hat and feather, after the style of the Jacobean period, an anachronism considered at that time of but little consequence. Above him stands an angel, "the genius of London," who bids him arise from his tomb. Forthwith he stands up, makes a congratulatory speech to the new mayor, and then "ridd on horsebacke with the rest of them," accompanied by representatives of the five citizens who were knighted along with him for their services against the rebels in Smithfield. From the time when the pageants were discontinued in 1702, the show sank down into a mere procession, with banners, music, the companies in their liveries, and the men in armour, as they have come down to our day. Hogarth gives us, in his series of *Idleness and Industry*, a graphic representation of the show of 1750, with the Prince and Princess of Wales seated under a canopy at the end of Paternoster Row.

A.D. 1643. Cheapside was one of the nine resting-places of the body of Eleanor of Castile, Queen of Edward I., on its progress from Lincolnshire to Westminster for burial, and here, opposite Wood Street, was erected, by Master Michael, a Canterbury mason, one of her beautiful memorial crosses. It fell to decay, and in 1441 was rebuilt with a conduit or fountain connected with it, but was not completely finished until the accession of Henry VII. The fanaticism of the Puritans after the Reformation caused them to look upon it and its statues of Jesus Christ, the Virgin, the Apostles, and a figure which they presumed to be, and which probably was, the effigy of a pope, with feelings of superstitious horror, and on several occasions they defaced the images and otherwise mutilated the cross. At length the reign of the Puritans commenced, and in 1643 the Parliament decreed its destruction, deputing one Robert Harlow to see it carried out. Accordingly in May of that year he filled Cheapside with a troop of horse, two companies of foot, and a body of workmen with ladders, picks, crowbars, and hammers, and as the official report informs us :—" On the 2nd of May, 1643, the cross in Cheapside was pulled down. At the fall of the top cross, drums beat, trumpets blew, and multitudes of caps were thrown in the air, and a great shout of people with joy. The 2nd of May, the Almanack says, was the invention of the cross, and the same day, at night, were the leaden popes burnt in the place where it stood, with ringing of bells and great acclamation, and no hurt at all done in these actions."

There is a print extant of the demolition of the cross, with workmen on ladders, hammering at the statues, and two men pulling down the finial cross with ropes, with a surrounding of horsemen, and beyond a body of troops with banners and uplifted weapons. A copy of the print is given in *Old and New London*, vol. i., p. 331.

In connection with that event a multitude of pamphlets appeared on both sides of the question, which may be seen in the Guildhall Library.

From the mass we select two for notice, the former especially as showing that the Cheapside 'prentices were then a power in the city worthy of being courted by flattery and adulation. Generally they adhered to the Puritanical side, but it would appear that there were some amongst them who held opposite views, from their coming forth with their clubs to prevent the demolition of the Cross; or it may be that they looked upon their Cross as a sort of palladium: had come to venerate it, and not being so bigoted as some of the Puritans, did not care to see it demolished. The title of the pamphlet runs thus:—" The Doleful lamentation of Cheapside Crosse: or, Old England sick of the Staggers: Together with the hearty thanks, which I, Jasper Crosse, hath lately returned to those noble-minded and gentele-bred 'prentices thereabouts, for rescuing my honour from being ravished, especially to Robert York, who was my chief protector at that time. London, 1641."

The second pamphlet, dated 1643, is entitled, " The Downfall of Dagon; or, the Taking Downe of Cheapside Crosse, the 2nd of May, 1643. Wherein is contained these principalls following, viz.: 1. Cheapside Crosse sick at the heart. 2. His death and funerall. 3. His will, legacies, inventory, and epitaph. 4. The reason why it was taken down, and the authority for it. 5. The benefit and profite that is made of the materialls of it, and the severall summes of money which is offered for it. Likewise the satisfaction it will give to thousands of people. 6. Notes worthy of the reader's observation that the crosse should just happen to bee taken downe on that day which crosses were first invented and set up."

We have now brought down the annals of Cheapside to comparatively modern and more prosaic times.

We no longer see the splendid pageantry and quaint festivities of the Norman, Plantagenet, and Tudor eras, with their bonfires, cresset-bearers, morrice-dancers, mummers, allegorical pageants, and house-fronts hung with tapestries, and other such textures. The joust, and tournaments, the setting of the Midsummer watch, and other curious and picturesque spectacles, are things of the past. It is true we still have the Lord Mayor's Show, and the procession to Westminster, but passing along the embankment instead of in the civic barges. We still retain the men in armour and the old gilt coach, and have representatives of the city companies in olden-time costumes, and we sometimes introduce novelties, such as a group of elephants mounted by " Africans."

Bishopsgate Street Within and Without.

SOME fourteen or fifteen centuries ago what is now Bishopsgate Street Within was a fashionable suburb of the Roman Londinium, the Belgravia or South Kensington of the period, where the aristocracy and wealth of the City located itself and built magnificent mansions after the fashion of Rome, with columns, frescoes, and tesselated pavements, such as we see in the disinterred city of Pompeii. In the streets might then be seen charioteers driving rapidly along to contend in the chariot race; fair ladies going to witness the gladiatorial displays in the amphitheatre; bronzed soldiers from many a distant province of the empire; slaves groaning beneath heavy burdens or employed in laborious occupations—all mixed up with the ordinary traffic of a considerable city. Northward, stretching eastward and westward, ran the City wall, a portion of which may still be seen in the street call London Wall, adorned with stately towers and bastions, one of the latter having been exposed to public view by the opening of a pathway through St. Giles's Churchyard. There was, however, no gateway in this part of the wall, as beyond lay an untraversable morass, and beyond that a forest extending to and up the heights of Highgate, Muswell Hill, etc., those who wished to go northward from the city having to go eastward to Aldgate or westward to Aldersgate. This probably was the reason why the rich selected this portion of the environs of the City for their residence, as being more retired and quiet than in the vicinity of a thoroughfare leading to a City outlet.

Of these mansions of the patricians of Londinium several vestiges have been found. On the site of St. Helen's, the foundations of large edifices have been laid bare. In 1707, at the corner of Camomile Street, a fine tesselated pavement was found; in 1752 another at the side of St. Helen's Gateway; in 1761 another in Camomile Street; and in 1836 a splendid specimen, in red, white, and grey, at the north-west angle of Crosby Square, besides fragments elsewhere.

This, however, was only in the later period of the Roman rule. When they had subdued the

Trinobantes, they found the capital of the country, although a place of commercial importance, merely a scattered collection of round huts with trackways in the midst, extending from Tower Hill to the Fleet River and from the Thames to Cheapside and Cornhill, defended on the north by earthworks, felled trees, and a ditch; and in midst of these huts they erected more substantial houses, with towers at the eastern and western extremities, and probably a temple to Diana, where St. Paul's Cathedral now stands. The northern outskirts, now Bishopsgate Street Within was appropriated as a burial-place, as they never buried their dead in the midst of the living; but in process of time the exigencies of the increasing population demanded an extension of the City boundaries, and they built over the old grave-yard, making a new cemetery on the site of the modern Bishopsgate Street Without, Shoreditch, and the fenlands lying eastward and westward of these. In 1576, when digging for clay near where Christ Church, Spitalfields, now stands, a great number of cinerary urns were found, containing burnt human remains, and in each a piece of coin, wherewith to pay Charon for ferrying the defunct across the Styx ; also, as Stow says, "divers vials and other old-fashioned glasses most cunningly wrought, such as I have not seen the like of, all which had water in them, differing from spring water" *(lachrymatories),* " cups and dishes of red earthenware and three or four images of white earth, about a span long, one of Pallas." Under the Camomile tesselated pavement, found in 1706, lay two feet of rubbish, and beneath that several funeral urns. Stone and timber coffins have also been found, or rather the nails of the latter, a quarter of a yard long, the wood having perished, and a Roman vault in St Botolph's Churchyard, all these, with skeletons or decayed bones in them, indicating burial after Christianity had become the religion of the empire, when the custom of burning the dead was abandoned.

The Saxons despised the effeminacy of decorated architecture and luxurious appliances in the way of household furniture, hence when they came into possession of London they allowed the sumptuous dwellings of the Romans to fall into decay and crumble to dust, preferring their own rough and uncomely habitations built of wood, but afterwards built their churches, monasteries, and public buildings generally of stone, and thus Roman London passed away.

The Saxons found it necessary to have another exit from the city northward between Aldgate and Aldersgate Street, and pierced the wall at the end of the street running from the river, whatever it may then have been called, and erected there a new gate. Erkenwald, Bishop of London, 679-97, has been credited with the work, but as this is only based upon the discovery, near by, of the statue of a mitred bishop, which it was presumed represented St. Erkenwald, the tradition may be doubted, but it was unquestionably this supposition which gave it the name of Bishops' Gate.

There are four churches in London dedicated to St. Botolph "the Briton," all situated by gates, Aldgate, Aldersgate, Billingsgate, and Bishopsgate. The latter lays claim to having been founded by the ancient British Christians, but, more probably, was built by the Saxons and dedicated to the British monk St. Botolph. It has been rebuilt no doubt several times since then. It escaped the ravages of the fire of 1666, but having become very much dilapidated, an Act of Parliament was obtained at the beginning of the last century for rebuilding it, by means of a rate of two shillings in the pound upon all household property in the parish, payable by the landlords, but this proving insufficient a parish rate was laid to supply the deficiency. It was commenced in 1725, and re-opened in 1728, having cost (there is nothing like precision) £10,444 1s. 8½d.

Tradition says that it was the burial-place of a brother of King Lud. The present building contains the tombs of Sir Paul Pinder; Edward Alleyn, the founder of Dulwich College; William, Earl of Devonshire, from whom Devonshire Square takes its name; and in the churchyard lies Hodges Shoughshware, "the chiefest servant of the King of Persia, who came from the King of Persia and died in his service, 1626, and Maghmote, his wife." The epitaph is in Persian, and entreats that all Persians who may read it will pray for their souls.

The Rev. Stephen Gorson, author of *The School of Abuse*, was rector of St. Botolph.

The venerable church of St. Helen is situated on the eastern side of the street, standing back and approached by an archway. Popular tradition ascribes its origin to the Emperor Constantine in honour of his mother, which is

G

doubtless an error, but it unquestionably dates from the Saxon age, as in 1010 the relics of King Edmund the Martyr were temporarily deposited within its walls, when brought from East Anglia, to prevent their desecration at the hands of the Danes. In the twelfth century the advowson appears to have been held by one Ranulph, as in the reign of Henry II., *circa* 1180, he and his son, Robert Fitz-Ranulph, made a grant of it to the Dean and Chapter of St. Paul's Cathedral. About half a century later, *circa* 1212, William Fitz-William, a London goldsmith, and ancestor of the extant Earls Fitzwilliam, founded in connection with it a priory for nuns of the order of St. Benedict, which was dedicated to the Holy Cross and St. Helen, the prioress on her election to swear fealty to the Dean and Chapter, who transferred to the priory the advowson of the church.

The church seems originally to have had simply a chancel and nave, without transepts or aisles, but when the priory was attached, it was duplicated by building another nave, and thus presented the appearance of a double-aisled church without an intermediate nave. A wall of division ran along the middle, one of the aisles being appropriated to the parishioners and the other to the nuns. It is to be feared that the fair inmates of the nunnery were not always very strict in their devotional exercises and seclusion from the outer world, and were even sometimes so naughty as to be subjected to punishments, one of which was being shut up in the crypt, which still exists, with the gratings, through which they could hear the service of the church without being present. Reginald Kentwode, dean of St. Paul's, in his periodical visitations, found so many "defautes and excesses" that he felt constrained to draw up a fresh code of rules for the regulation of the house, the original of which is amongst the Cotton MSS. in the British Museum.

Willyam Basynge, Sheriff of London, 1309, added considerably to the buildings, and came to be regarded as the second founder.

The seal of the priory was an oval, representing the Empress Helena standing by the cross (which she found in the Holy Land and brought to Europe) with the nails in her hand, and on the opposite side worshippers in the act of adoration. An impression of it is pendant from a deed in the possession of the Leathersellers' Company, and an engraving of it is given in Malcolm's *London Rediv.*, vol. iii., p. 548.

At the dissolution of the priory the site was given to Richard Williams, one of the visitors of the monasteries, in exchange for certain lands in Huntingdonshire. He assumed the name of Cromwell, being a kinsman of Cromwell, Earl of Essex, and was ancestor of the Protector, Oliver Cromwell. The dividing wall in the church was taken down and the whole of the space appropriated to the use of the parishioners. The Leathersellers purchased the nuns' hall, and made it the hall of their company. The priory buildings remained, but in a ruined state, until 1799, when they were cleared away, and St. Helen's Place built on the site. A view of the ruins is given in Wilkinson's *Londina Illustrata*, and a picturesque view of the church and the Leathersellers' Hall in Malcolm's *London Rediv.*, 1803.

The church contained more "altar" tombs with recumbent and kneeling effigies than any other church in the City, but they suffered terrible mutilation from the iconoclastic zeal of the Puritans, many of them having been altogether destroyed. Sir Thomas Gresham had promised to build a tower, which unhappily he was prevented doing by death, and it was not until 1699, that it was furnished with a steeple. The church has undergone many repairs and restorations, notably by Inigo Jones, 1623-4, and frequently in the plaster and whitewash style of decoration. The last and most judicious restoration was carried out in 1867-8, and the venerable old church may now be seen, after weathering so many storms, with its graceful Gothic arches, its groupings of tombs and monuments, the nuns' grating in the crypt, its grotesque heads, and over one of the doors the black figure of St. Helena, for which hundreds of pounds have been offered by foreign Catholics, and refused; with many of the same features that were looked at by the Greshams, the Crosbys, and other old parishioners of the Norman, Plantagenet, and Tudor ages, with the addition of some modern stained windows and an organ built in 1742, and rebuilt in 1868. The rectory was sold by Queen Elizabeth to Michael and Edward Stanhope, with the proviso of paying a stipend of £20 per annum to a vicar. Amongst the tombs are those of Sir Thomas Gresham, a splendid monument; Sir John Crosby, in full armour, and his wife, one of the oldest remaining; Sir John Lawrence, the noble Lord Mayor of the Plague year; Sir John Spencer, "Rich Spencer," whose daughter and heiress eloped with her lover, Compton, in a baker's basket.

St. Ethelburga is a small and very ancient church, squeezed almost out of sight by intervening parasitic shops; when or by whom founded not known, but most probably in the Saxon age. In an old print it is represented with a spire similar to that in Langham Place. It escaped the fire of 1666, was repaired and "beautified" in 1694, and again in 1701. St. Ethelburga was the daughter of Ethelbert, the first Christian king of Kent, and patron of St. Augustine; she married Eadwine, King of Northumbria, the convert of St Paulinus, after whose death, in battle at the hands of Penda, the Pagan king of Mercia, she fled with her children and Paulinus to her brother, who had succeeded to the kingdom of Kent, and who nominated Paulinus to the see of Rochester.

Walter Brune, citizen, and Rosia, his wife, in 1235, founded a priory of canons and hospital for the sick and needy, dedicated to our blessed Mary, called St. Mary Spital Without, Bishopsgate. It was suppressed in 1539, at which time it made up 180 beds, and supplied the sick occupants with all necessaries at a cost of £478 per annum. Outside was the pulpit where the famous Spital sermons were preached at Easter before the Mayor and Corporation, and sometimes royal personages, by the most eminent City divines. After the dissolution they were preached at St. Paul's, then in St. Bride's Church, and now in Christ Church, Newgate Street. The pulpit stood on a site that now forms the north-east corner of Spital Square. There existed for 120 years in the precincts of Bishopsgate, near Camomile Street, a curious fraternity called The Papey, a religious house of St. John and St. Charity, sometimes called St. Augustine's Papey, consisting of threescore priests, governed by a master and two wardens. Its objects were to supply the necessities of the poorer clergy by providing them with lodgings, coals, bread, and ale. Near by stood the church of St. Augustine-in-the-Wall, the patronage of which was vested in the rich Priory of the Holy Trinity, who presented to the living four rectors from 1321 to 1375, but after that no one could be found to accept the incumbency in consequence of the stinginess of the Priory—the stipend not being sufficient to live upon—who therefore in 1430 gave the church to the Papey guild. The fraternity was not rich in funds, and in order to improve their exchequer they practised the singing of dirges and attended funerals as professional mourners and dirge singers. The house was suppressed 2 Edwd. VI.

From the thirteenth to the seventeenth century a conspicuous feature in the line of road leading northward from Bishopsgate was the Priory of Bethlehem, with its square-towered church, its gabled houses for the brethren and sisters' habitations, and its gardens, situated at the eastern edge of the moorland of Fensbury, a little beyond St. Botolph's Church, and facing what are now New Street and Devonshire Place. It was then built quite in the country, with the fens behind, fields in front, and no houses beyond it. The roadway in front was nothing more than a beaten trackway, almost impassable in winter, which when houses came to be built along it, and it assumed the semblance of a street, was called Bedlam Gate. There is no view extant of the priory, excepting the bird's-eye view in Aggas' Map, *temp.* Elizabeth, where there is a continuous line of houses along Bedlam Gate and onward to St. Leonard's Church, Shoreditch, where the road apparently terminated; eastward is the Spittel Fyeld, with archers and cattle; and westward, Finsburie Fyeld, with windmills, bowmen practising at the butts, and women spreading out linen to dry.

The priory was founded in 1246 by Simon Fitz-Marie, sheriff of London in the same year, for brethren and sisters, canons of the Order of the Star of Bethlehem, subject to the Bishop of Bethlehem, to whom they had to pay one mark yearly at Easter. Their habit was a black gown with a star embroidered on the breast. When it became a hospital for lunatics is not known, but there are records of sick persons being nursed there in 1330, and of insane patients in 1403, when six of the latter and three of the former were maintained in the house. Weaver tells us that at one time there was "a house for distraught and lunaticke people" at Charing Cross, and that some king, he did not know who, not liking to have an establishment of people of that class so near his palace, packed them off to Bethlem Priory, which was probably the beginning of its career as a hospital for the insane.

The Hospital-Priory does not appear to have been very amply provided with funds, as in 1403 some of the houses were alienated, for the purpose seemingly of raising money, and the brethren had to go abroad collecting alms for the sustenance of the inmates. In 1523, one Stephen Gunnings, a merchant tailor, left £40 in trust to the Corporation for purchasing the house, to be continued as a receptacle for lunatics, and the Mayor took some steps for that purpose; but before they were carried out it was granted to the Corporation, after the Dissolution, by King Henry VIII., who placed it in charge of the governors of Christ's Hospital in 1556, and the following year transferred it to the governors of Bridewell. In 1555 the income, arising chiefly out of rents, amounted to £43 4s. 8d. per annum, and by 1632 they were valued at £470, which, not being all forthcoming, was inadequate for the support of the house, and the Spital preachers were directed to appeal to their hearers on its behalf, there being then forty-four lunatics within the walls, the revenues paying only two-thirds of the cost of their maintenance. Besides, there were so many pressing cases for admission, that it became necessary to discharge many of the half-cured and less violent patients, to whom were granted licences for begging, and they went abroad, dressed fantastically, singing "mad songs," and imploring food or money. They went by the name of "Tom o' Bedlams," and are alluded to by Shakespeare in *King Lear*, where he says—

"With a sigh like Tom o' Bedlam."

In the reign of Elizabeth the church and chapel were taken down, and houses built on the site; and in the following century, the buildings having become ruinous and much too small for the constantly increasing patients, it was resolved to build a new and larger hospital. The Corporation made a grant of land on the southern margin of Finsbury Moors, where the Liverpool Street railway stations now stand, and the public contributed £17,000 towards its erection. It was commenced in 1644, and completed in 1676; and in 1732 two wings were added, which made the entire length of the building 540 feet, with a depth of forty feet. The style adopted was that of the Tuileries in Paris, which so offended Louis XIV. that he caused some out-offices of a more useful and less dignified character to be built in the style of St. James's Palace, London. It was adorned with figures of raving and melancholy madness from the chisel of Caius Cibber, which are now in the hall of the present hospital.

The estates belonging to the hospital afterwards rapidly increased in value, and at the beginning of the present century the governors found themselves in a position to build a larger and better-planned building, and purchased a large plot of land in St. George's Fields, which with the new hospital cost £100,000. The total income is now about £20,000 per annum.

Until towards the end of the last century the insane were treated in a most barbarous way. Nakedness, chains, scourgings, and solitary confinement were their lot, calculated rather to intensify than alleviate their aberration of intellect, without any of the modern appliances of modern asylums—music, flowers, prints, books, amusements, cheerful society, and comparative liberty—which are now found to be essential towards their recovery. A good idea of the old style of madhouse may be obtained from the eighth plate of Hogarth's series of "The Rake's Progress," which represents a scene in the Moorfields Bedlam.

A few years ago a skeleton of a dwarf with

fetters on the legs was dug up near Bishopsgate, supposed to be that of a patient of Bedlam. The road in front of the second hospital was formerly called "Old Bethlem" and was changed to Liverpool Street in honour of Lord Liverpool, Prime Minister 1812-27.

The Hon. Artillery Company, which originated here, removed to the present Artillery Ground in City Road in 1622, and has numbered amongst its officers Charles II., when Prince of Wales; James II., when Duke of York, after the Restoration; and George IV., when Prince of Wales, as Captain in Command. The old Artillery Ground in Bishopsgate Street has left reminiscences of its existence in the names of Artillery Lane, Artillery Passage, Gun Street, and Fort Street.

From a very remote period has the company of Leathersellers been connected with Bishopsgate Street and its vicinity. In the Norman age the tanners, curriers, and leather dressers clustered about Cripplegate and further eastward, where the stream of Walbrook entered the City, that locality being the Bermondsey of the period. The Company is supposed to have been formed in the Saxon times, but little or nothing is known of it until 1372, when the wardens and seniors presented a petition to the Corporation praying that stringent measures might be put in force against fraudulent craftsmen who used inferior dyes for staining their skins. They were incorporated in 1397-8, and were re-incorporated by Henry VI. in 1444, with power to elect four wardens and fifteen members of the court, and to use a seal with arms. The charter is a magnificent specimen of penmanship, and beautifully illuminated. There is a picture extant of the king presenting the charter to the four kneeling wardens in livery dresses of red and blue, furred at the edges, descending to the knees, and fastened at the waist with a girdle garnished with white metal. By this charter they were empowered to regulate the mystery in London, which powers were enlarged by Henry VII., who extended their supervision of the trade throughout the kingdom. In 1604 James I. granted them a new charter, which, like that of Henry VI., is a wonderfully fine specimen of art, with an emblazonry of the company's arms and an illumination of eight liverymen in their robes of office—black gowns trimmed with " foins," hoods of scarlet, and black flat caps.

The first hall of the company was built in 1445, in the parish of All Saints' by the Wall, south of the present Finsbury Circus, where now stand Leathersellers' Buildings. A century after it became too small, and a portion of the site and buildings of the dissolved priory of St. Helen was purchased in 1543, and the nuns' hall converted into that of the company, which, with alterations and embellishments, came to be for a long time the finest livery hall in London. The ceiling was enriched with beautiful pendants, and at the end was a splendid Elizabethan screen, elaborately decorated. In the courtyard was a pump with the figure of a mermaid, from whose breast issued wine on gala occasions. It was the work of Cibber, who gave it in 1679, in payment of his admission fee to the membership of the company.

In 1799 the hall was sold along with other of the priory buildings, to clear the site for the building of St. Helen's Place. A new hall was built on the same site, but with new fittings, all the antique decorations of the old hall having been disposed of. This, the third hall, was destroyed by fire in 1819, the valuable collection of records being fortunately saved, and the present hall, occupying the north-east corner of St. Helen's Place, was built 1820-22.

The first record book of the company commences November 12th, 1472, with the following as the earliest entry :—

> "Wyllyam J. Curtes gave to us this boke,
>   For to regystre every wardenn's tyme in ;
> Pray for hym when ye doe loke,
> That God will reward hym. Amen."

There are almshouses of the company in Clarke's Court, St. Helen's: White's Alley, Coleman Street ; and Hart Street, Cripplegate.

Excepting the Borough High Street, perhaps no street in London had so many famous old inns, with galleried court-yards, cross-timbered walls, quaint gables, and latticed windows, as Bishopsgate Street, established for the accommodation of carriers and travellers from the north-eastern towns. Amongst them were the White Hart; formerly the Magpie, which stood by the gateway of Bethlem Priory, supposed to have been originally the hostelry of the priory, afterwards an inn for travellers who arrived after the gate was shut for the night. It seems, from a date on the wall, to have been rebuilt in 1480, and was standing in 1810, when a view was taken representing it with a double range of bay windows. It was again rebuilt in 1829, and stood at the corner of Liverpool Street. The Bull, where Burbage and his companions obtained a patent from Queen Elizabeth for the performance of theatricals in the quadrangle, the spectators occupying the surrounding galleries. This was the inn to which old Hobson, the Cambridge carrier, resorted, from whom came the saying of " Hobson's choice "—that or none. On a wall of the inn was his effigy, in fresco, clutching a money bag, with an inscription—" The fruitful mother of a hundred more."

The Green Dragon, an old Tudor house. The Catherine Wheel still a carriers' house. The King's Head, at the corner of Spital Square. The Wrestlers, a large inn, and the Angel, were in existence *temp.* Henry VI. The City of London Tavern, with pillared facade, famous in modern times for its public dinners, was converted, in 1839, into the Wesleyan Centenary Hall, established in commemoration of the centennial year of the formation of the Society of Methodists.

On the eastern side of the street, within and near to the gate, were certain tenements belonging to a fraternity of St. Nicholas, which were given (27 Henry VI.) to the Company of Parish Clerks for the maintenance of two chaplains in the Chapel of St. Mary Magdalene, near the Guildhall, and behind these stood the hall of the Parish Clerks, and seven almshouses for the poor, to one of whom was given sixteenpence and the other six ninepence per week.

The Post-office, which had been in Cloak Lane, Dowgate, was removed after the fire of 1666, to the Black Swan, in Bishopsgate Street, whence it was removed to Lombard Street, and subsequently to St. Martin-le-Grand.

We have noticed the palatial character of the Bishopsgate quarter of Roman Londinum, vestiges of its splendour having been frequently disinterred in recent times, in attestation of the fact. A thousand years afterwards it again became a district of sumptuous mansions—palaces, not of the Roman patricians, but of the merchant princes of the modern metropolis of the world. Most fortunately, the ravages of the great fire of '66 only extended to the borders of the ward, and thus have been preserved to us those precious architectural relics of Crosby House; and the churches of St. Helen and St. Ethelburga. The quaint old house of Sir Paul Pindar, has just been taken down.

Sir John Crosby was born *circa* 1420, and died in 1475; he was a grocer (a wholesale merchant) and woolman, and at one time Mayor of the Staple at Calais. He was elected an alderman in 1465; served the office of sheriff in 1471, in which year he was knighted by Edward IV., and represented the City in Parliament in the year 1461. He was a zealous Yorkist, in high favour with Edward IV., particularly distinguished himself in the defence of the City against the Lancastrian admiral, the Bastard of Fauconbridge, and is introduced by Heywood, in his drama of *King Edward IV.* In 1466 he took on lease from the Prioress of St. Helen's certain tenements for a period of ninety-nine years, at a rent of £11 6s. 8d. per annum, which he demolished, and built on the site " ye highest and fairest house in ye citie," which he did not enjoy long, as it was only completed four years before his death. Of its grandeur we may form some conception from what remains of it after the fire of 1674, especially the great hall, fifty-four feet long, twenty-seven and a half feet broad, and forty feet high, with its oriel windows eleven feet in breadth, and extending from the floor to the ceiling, and its timbered roof of surpassing beauty. Around this old mansion many most interesting historical associations have clustered. Richard, Duke of Gloucester, inhabited it for some time, and it figures in Shakespeare's pages as the place where he concocted his plot for the murder of his nephews, his marriage with his niece, which he could not accomplish, and the usurpation of the throne. From 1516 to 1523, it was the abode of Sir Thomas More, where it is supposed he wrote his *Utopia*.

It has been occupied by several aldermen, some of whom held their mayoralty there, amongst others, Alderman Bond, who added a turret to the building; Sir John Spencer, who built a large warehouse behind it; Sir Bartholomew Read, Lord Mayor, who entertained Catherine of Arragon for two or three days within its walls, previous to her marriage with Prince Arthur. The Emperor Maximilian lodged there when in London in 1502; Queen Elizabeth came there in 1594 to witness a masque by some law students, and the famous Countess of Pembroke made it her residence for some time, where it is probable Shakespeare visited her. During the Civil War it was made a prison for captured Royalists, after which the great hall was converted into a Presbyterian chapel. In 1678 the drawing-room and throne room were used as warehouses by the East India Company, and afterwards as a packer's workrooms, when they sustained a great deal of mutilation. In 1831, it was advertised to be sold for demolition, but some spirited persons came forward and rescued it from that fate, besides restoring and repairing it. From 1842 to 1860 it was a literary institute, and is now a restaurant. the proprietor having with great good taste preserved all the old features, and in the necessary additional buildings has adhered to the same style. It is supposed to have consisted originally of two quadrangles, separated by the great hall, and that it had a facade of 100 feet in length to Bishopsgate Street.

Sir John gave 500 marks towards the restoration of St. Helen's Church, and his arms were placed on the walls and in the windows. He was thrice married, and had an only son, who died without issue, the line thus becoming extinct.

Sir Paul Pindar was a notable merchant and diplomatist, minister of James I. in Turkey, who was born about the end of the sixteenth or beginning of the seventeenth century, and died in 1650. On his return from Turkey he brought with him a diamond valued at £30,000, which the king wished to purchase "on tick," but the cautious merchant, not having sufficient confidence in his credit, declined to let him have it on those terms. However, he agreed to lend it to him to flash it in the eyes of his subjects on State occasions. He afterwards sold it to Charles I., but most probably was never paid for it. He was reputed to have been worth a quarter of a million sterling at one time, an enormous sum for that period. He gave £18,000 towards the repairs of St. Paul's Cathedral, and expended other sums on charitable and philanthropic objects, but although so wealthy he lost so much money in bad debts, arising out of loans to Kings James I. and Charles I. that he fell into comparative poverty, and died in debt himself.

He erected for his residence a magnificent house on the western side of the street, without the gate, a portion of whose picturesque frontal remaining in 1890, attracted the notice and admiration of every passer-by. It was a fine specimen of Elizabethan architecture, and richly decorated both without and within. There were rooms with wainscoted walls, sculptured chimney-pieces, and ceilings profusely ornamented, but most of them terribly mutilated; one splendid ceiling represented the sacrifice of Isaac, with a radiation of beautiful ornamentation. Behind the house was a park, with mulberry trees, some of which were only cut down within the present century; and near by, in Halfmoon Alley, stood a house, with sculptural details, which is supposed to have been the gatekeeper's lodge. A small portion with a narrow frontage was converted into a tavern, with the sign of the Sir Paul Pindar, which has just been taken down by the Great Eastern Railway.

Devonshire House.—Built by one Jasper Fisher, around which he laid out extensive pleasure grounds. It was held by the Cavendishes until 1670, but in the interval, during the ascendency of the Puritans, had been taken possession of by them, and made use of as a chapel. Butler, in his *Hudibras*, describes the Rump Parliament as like—

"No part of the nation
But Fisher's folly congregation."

After this it was opened as a "Bank of Credit," a sort of pawnshop, which did not last long, as by 1708, Devonshire Square was built, described by Hatton as "a pretty, though very small square, inhabited by gentry and other merchants."

Sir Thomas Gresham, the wealthy and munificent founder of the Royal Exchange, was born *circa* 1519; died, 1579; was knighted, 1559; married Anne, daughter of William Fernley, and relict of William Read, and had issue an only son, Richard, who died v.p. and s.p. 1564.

He was a parishioner of St. Helen's, and in that parish he built his house, which Stow describes as "the most spacious thereabouts, builded of brick and timber," and that is about all he could say in eulogy of it, for it appears, from engravings of it, to have been more remarkable for size than for architectural grandeur. It was built in the Flemish style, chiefly by Flemish workmen, and extended from the west side of Bishopsgate Street to Broad Street. It consisted of a quadrangle of two galleried stories, with gabled attics; a piazza and rows of trees running round, giving it a quiet, collegiate air, and a picturesque aspect, and was surrounded by gardens and pleasure grounds, with trees. It was commenced about the year 1559, and was finished in 1562. Within its walls Sir Thomas entertained Queen Elizabeth, and had the custody of the Lady Mary Grey.

At his death he left it to his widow for life, and at her decease in trust to the Corporation of London and the Mercers' Company, to be converted into a College of Professors, with salaries of £50 per annum, to lecture weekly on divinity, astronomy, music, law, geometry, medicine, and rhetoric, for the gratuitous instruction of the young citizens of London, which were commenced in 1597. Amongst the professors were several eminent men, one of whom was Sir Christopher Wren, who, in conjunction with others, there laid the foundation of the Royal Society. The trustees allotted two rooms to the Society, one for their meetings, the other for their books and philosophical instruments. Pepys tells of King Charles making merry over the people of Gresham House, and Boyle in particular, amusing themselves with the child's play of weighing air. The society met at Gresham House until 1710, when they removed to Crane Court.

After the Great Fire of 1666, when nearly all

the public buildings were destroyed, Gresham House became the Mansion House and residence of the Lord Mayor, the Law Courts, and the Exchange, the merchants assembling in the quadrangle, where they remained until their establishments were rebuilt.

The collegiate lectures were not properly appreciated, and became almost sinecures to the professors, until in 1768-70 the Government, wanting an excise office in the City, agreed with the trustees to take a perpetual lease of the site, at the absurdly low rental of £500 per annum, the trustees to take down the buildings, to do which cost them £1,800. The lectures were then removed to a dull, upper room in the Exchange, where they were delivered until the destruction of the Exchange by fire, in 1838, when they were given in the City of London School, until the opening of the New Gresham Lecture Hall, in Basinghall Street, in 1843.

Dashwood House stood westward of St. Botolph's Churchyard, and was the City mansion of the Dashwood family; afterwards it is supposed to have been the residence of Lady Jane Grey. It was subsequently converted into the Ottoman Bank, and Consular and Mercantile

Offices; has recently been taken down, and a colossal block constructed for suites of offices.

There are many other fine old houses in the ward, dating from before the Fire, whose fronts have been modernised by building up the space beneath the overhanging upper floors and removing the gables, but which retain many of their olden time features at their backs, and are still adorned in their interiors with fine balustraded staircases, carved chimney pieces, and timber-work ceilings.

Another house of a somewhat different but very useful character stood in Bishopsgate Street. In 1649 the Corporation of London founded a house called the London Workhouse, "for the entertainment of the greatest objects of commiseration, but likewise to receive a great number of the miserable and unhappy vagrant orphans known by the infamous name of 'blackguard,' the pest and shame of the City, pilfering and begging about the streets by day, and lying therein, almost naked, in all seasons of the year by night." In 1662 a charter of incorporation was granted, under the name of "The President (always the Lord Mayor) and Governors of the Poor of the City of London." In 1700 a large house was built for the reception of these objects of charity, and in 1704 it is recorded that " 368 children were fed, clothed, and taught to work and the principles of religion;" besides whom there were " maintained and employed 653 vagabonds, sturdy beggars, and other idle and disorderly persons." It was taken down early in the present century, the Poor law administration rendering it superfluous.

In the Parish of St. Helen's there lived and died a man of eccentric opinions and evil reputation, very different in character from his neighbours, the merchant princes of Bishopsgate. His name was Francis Bancroft, and his vocation that of a summoning officer in the Lord Mayor's Court, in which capacity he made a large fortune by issuing false summonses, "not only pillaging the poor, but likewise many of the rich, who, rather than lose time in appearing before the said magistrate, gave money to get rid of this common pest of the citizens." He was so much detested that at his funeral the populace nearly jostled his coffin off the shoulders of the bearers, and they set the bells ringing "for joy at his unlamented death."

He entertained an eccentric notion that in a

certain number of years after his death he should return to life and occupy his original position in the City, and in accordance with this idea had a vault, with folding doors and glass in the panels, constructed in St. Helen's Church, and a coffin with hinges only, not screwed down, so that when he came to life he would have nothing to do but to step out of his coffin, open the doors of the vault, and walk out. His name is remembered by his having bequeathed £27,000 for the foundation of almshouses for twenty-four poor almsmen, a chapel, a school for one hundred poor boys, and houses for two masters. The money was left in trust to the Drapers' Company, who erected the buildings at Mile-end in 1735. There was a proviso in the will that the trustees should visit his tomb and look upon his body, in May every year for ever, failing which the money to be diverted to other purposes. They have long discontinued the custom, but still hold the trust, and although the testator has now lain 150 years in his unfastened coffin, he has not come forth yet to rectify this direliction of duty on the part of the Drapers.

From a very early period has Bishopsgate Street and Ward been a centre of Nonconformity.

Maitland, writing 1725-36, refers to three Presbyterian, two Independents, and one Quaker's meeting houses in the parishes of St Botolph and St. Helen. The Devonshire Square Baptist church was, excepting one in Kent, the oldest in England, and in its early years suffered much from persecution. It migrated hither from Wapping in 1638, and occupied a part of Devonshire House, or, as it was popularly called, Fisher's Folly. The chapel was built in 1653, which was taken possession of by the Episcopalians after the fire, and used for Church of England services until the churches of London were rebuilt. It continued to flourish until, the Metropolitian Railway requiring the site, it was taken down and a new Gothic chapel, with spire, built at Stoke Newington out of the proceeds of the sale, at a cost of £11,000. It has had several notable ministers, the most remarkable being William Kaffin, who made an eminent figure among the Antipœdo-Baptists of the 17th century.

Crosby Hall Independent Church. The Rev. Thos. Watson, whose chief work was "A body of Divinity," consisting of 176 sermons, fol., 1792, posth. Stephen Charnock, B.D. Benjamin

Grosvenor, D.D., a very eminent man, who held the pastorate from 1704 to 1749, one of the most popular preachers in London; and was also lecturer in the Old Jewry, at the Weigh House, and at Salters' Hall. Portrait in Dr. Williams' library. Edmund Calamy, B.D., son of Dr. Edm. Calamy, author of the "Nonconformist Memorial." On the expiration of the lease in 1799, the congregation was dispersed, and the chapel was rented by James Relly, a rough and uncultured Welshman, but a powerful preacher, who established a church of Rellyanists or Rellyan Universalists, who held a species of anti-nomian doctrine. He was author of some controversial works, now altogether forgotten.

A Presbyterian meeting-house was erected in Little St. Helen's in 1672, under the Indulgence, which became a place of importance in the annals of Nonconformity. Within its walls the first public ordination of Nonconformist ministers took place, and the Coward Lecture preached there from 1721, till the demolition of the chapel. There was also a seven o'clock morning lecture, preached every Sunday in the summer months, to commemorate the accession of the House of Hanover. The first minister, he who took out the licence and collected the congregation, was the learned and pious Samuel Annesley, LL.D., the ejected of St. Giles's Cripplegate, formerly rector of Cliffe, Kent, and of St. Matthew's, Friday Street, London, lecturer at St. Paul's, and one of the preachers at Whitehall during the Protectorate. He was first cousin to Arthur Annesley, Earl of Anglesey; was a popular preacher, and author of some published sermons and other works. He continued in the pastorate until his death in 1694. Anne, his daughter, a very superior woman in every respect, in piety, intelligence, and sound discretion, was married to the Rev. Samuel Wesley, vicar of Epworth, and bore him nineteen children, amongst whom were John and Charles Wesley, the founders of Methodism.

Benj. Robinson occupied the pulpit from 1701 to 1724, a Derbyshire man, of great reputation, and Merchant Lecturer at Salters' Hall. After him the church gradually dwindled down until 1790, when Mr. Brown preached there for two years, and removed with his congregation to Shoreditch; after whom Christian Frederick Trieber, with a Lutheran congregation, occupied it for two years, and on the expiration of the lease removed to

Cheapside. Some other ministers of various denominations preached in the chapel for short periods until 1799, when it was taken down and houses built on the site.

In Hand Alley, on the western side of Bishopsgate Without, stood a large Presbyterian meeting-house. On the site had been a plague pit, and when it was proposed to be built upon it, the bodies, some not entirely decomposed, 2,000 in number, were carted away and buried in another pit, over which is a passage to Rose Alley. The chapel was built soon after Bartholomew Day for Thomas Vincent, famous for his labours amongst the poor during the plague of 1665, who held the pastorate until his death in 1678. After the fire of 1666, his chapel was seized by the clergyman of a City parish, who performed service there until his church was rebuilt. After him came a succession of popular ministers, until the beginning of the 18th century, when the congregation, a wealthy body, removed with their minister, Dr. John Evans, author of "A Discourse on Temper," to a new chapel, which they built in 1727, in New Broad Street, when the old chapel was pulled down.

A Particular Baptist Church, in Great St.

Helens, existed during the time of the civil war, when the famous Hansard Knollys was the pastor. He was a Lincolnshire man of great oratorical talent, and gathered about him a congregation of a thousand hearers. His doctrines, however, were deemed irregular and unsound by the Presbyterians, and he was summoned before the Westminster assembly of divines, who prohibited him from preaching. This prohibition appears, however, to have been withdrawn afterwards, as from 1645 to 1691, he preached the doctrines in Curriers' Hall. He was author of " The Smoke of the Temple," "An Exposition of the Book of Revelations," and some other works, including an autobiography written in 1672. His death occurred in 1691, at the age of 93, when he was buried in Bunhill Fields. Portrait in Wilson's " History of the Dissenting Church."

The Society of Friends have a large meeting-house in Bishopsgate Street, which is the head quarters of the society, where the annual meetings are held, when Friends from all parts of England assemble here, giving quite a picturesque aspect to the street, when it is thronged by them in their somewhat grotesque costume. Their first meeting-house was in Bull and Mouth Street, Aldersgate, which was destroyed by the fire of '66, rebuilt and occupied till 1744, when they removed to White Hart Court, Gracechurch Street. Many of the members of this meeting were the originators of some of the most eminent banking firms of Lombard Street, such as the Gurneys, the Barclays, the Hoares, the Hanburys, the Lloyds, the Mastermans, the Jansons, the Osgoods, the Dimsdales, and others; and it was from there that the remains of George Fox were carried to Bunhill Fields for burial, followed by 3,000 Friends. This chapel becoming too small for the congregation, a new one, that now existing, was erected in Bishopsgate Street on the site of the Dolphin Inn.

In 1838 a Jews' synagogue was built in Great St. Helens. It is the largest in London in the Italian style, with a splendid interior.

The Wesleyan Centenary Hall stands in a commanding position opposite the end of Threadneedle Street, with a fine pedimented range of columns.

We have, in our historical retrospect, seen Bishopsgate under various aspects. In the Roman era, when it was a suburb of aristocratic residences, with all the appliances of Roman civilisation, and all the beauties of Roman art; in the Saxon and Norman periods, with its mean habitations and monastic establishments, with cowled monks, and bare-footed friars, conspicuous amongst the wayfarers as they passed along the thoroughfare ankle deep in mud, or blinded by the clouds of dust from the unpaved roads; in the days of the Tudors and Stuarts, when it was lined with picturesque gabled houses, with overhanging upper floors, cross timberings, and latticed windows; with quaint old hostelries and their galleried courtyards, frequently occupied by fashionable crowds of spectators, witnessing the performances of the actors of the Elizabethan drama; and with the noble mansions of the City magnates and merchant princes. In addition to these, there was the City gate and a conduit at each end of the street, one to the north, just within the gate, erected by Lord Mayor Knesworth in 1505; the other at the south end, at its junction with the streets of Cornhill, Leadenhall, and Gracious Church. The street was rendered more passable for pedestrians and vehicles by being paved in 1543, and the sloughs of despond, previously so characteristic of

London thoroughfares, and so impedimental to locomotion, got rid of. After this followed the Georgian or dark age of architecture, when the quaint old houses of the past were replaced by the hideous abortions of the last and beginning of the present century.

Now for the third time we see Bishopsgate Street again gradually assuming an aspect of architectural grandeur, which will make it in another fifty years one of the finest streets in London or any other city. Within the last few years there have been erected several blocks of buildings of a palatial character, and this process of transformation is still going on with great rapidity. Among the more notable we may mention the National and Provincial Bank of England, one of the finest buildings of Modern London; the Royal Bank Buildings, the London and Lancashire Life Office, the Capital and Counties Bank, the South Sea Chambers, the Palmerston Buildings, the Devonshire Chambers, the Royal Bank of Scotland, and the block of offices at the rear of St. Botolph's Church.

Aldersgate Street and St. Martin's-le-Grand.

THESE two streets, forming one continuous thoroughfare, are so intimately associated in their annals, that it is almost impossible to write the history of one of them without constant reference to the other.

Aldersgate Street derives its name from the old City gate which was the north-western outlet of the City, and St. Martin's-le-Grand (formerly Martin's Lane) from the collegiate establishment which occupied the site of the older or eastern portion of the Post Office. In the last century, that portion from the Barbican to the Bars was called "Pick-axe Street." Aldersgate is supposed to have been one of the four gates of Roman London, and was in the line of an ancient British trackway, improved by the Romans into a road called Watling Street, which came from Dover, crossed the Thames by a ferry, passed along where the modern Watling Street is, emerged from the City by Aldersgate, and went onwards towards Verulamium (St. Albans). As to the origin of the name there are various discrepant presumptions. Some assume that it was so called because it was one of the elder, or one of the four original gates; others that it obtained its name from a Saxon—one Aldrich, the builder or re-edifier of it; but the most probable assumption is that it was so denominated from the alder, or elder trees which grew in great profusion in that locality. The wall, after leaving Cripplegate, proceeded westward for a short distance, then turned at a sharp angle to the south, along the present Noble Street, until it came to near where the Castle and Falcon stands, where it again took a south-westerly direction, past St. Botolph's Church and the Greyfriars' Monastery. As represented by Aggas's map, there were four semicircular bastions in the Noble Street portion, looking westward, and two in the line from Noble Street to Greyfriars, besides the gate at the end of St. Martin's Lane, which is there represented as a heterogeneous mass of buildings, fortified, and with two posterns, the centre arch being hidden by a low building standing in front of it. A little to the north-west of Cripplegate stood a watch-tower called the Barbican, on the north side of the street bearing that name. It was erected by the Romans, and was garrisoned by a cohort of soldiers, who had a threefold duty to perform: first to keep an outlook for approaching enemies, secondly to watch for the outbreak of fire in the City, and thirdly to keep a beacon blazing on the top to serve as a guide for travellers by night over the northern fens and moors. Bridgewater House, which was destroyed by fire in 1698, is supposed to have been built on the site, and now Bridgewater Square. Some remains of the old Barbican were to be seen here in the last century.

Very little is known of the earlier history of Aldersgate. Stow says "This gate was antiently at divers times increased with buildings, namely on the south side, a great frame of timber was set up, containing many large rooms and lodgings; and on the east side was the addition of one large building of timber with one large floor, paved with stone or tile, and a well therein curbed with stone to a great depth, and rising into the said room two stories high from the ground."

In 1610, Thomas Hayes erected a conduit a

little way to the north of the gate, which was supplied with water brought in pipes from the Thames.

It was usual to grant the rooms over the gates as residences for officials of the Corporation, those over Aldersgate being generally appropriated to the city crier. There is among the Corporation Records a deed of grant, in Latin, dated 49, Edw. 3, 1378, which, translated, runs thus: "Be it remembered that we, William Walworth, Mayor of London and the Assembly of Aldermen, with the assent of the Commonality of the City aforesaid, by reason of the good service by Ralph Strode, Common Countor (pleader or common serjeant) unto us done and hereafter to be done, have given and granted unto the said Ralph all the dwelling houses, together with the garden and all other appurtenances, situate over the gate of Aldrichesgate, to have and to hold the same as long as he, the said Ralph, shall remain in the said office of Countor, it being understood that the Chamberlain for the time being during the next year shall cause at his own expense all and singular the defaults in the said house to be repaired, etc." In the reign of Elizabeth it was occupied by the famous printer, John Day. Frequently, as was usual with city gates, Aldersgate presented to the view of passers-by a ghastly garnishing of the dismembered limbs of traitors. Thus Pepys writes, October 20th, 1660: "This afternoon, going through London and calling at Crowe's (Alderman Crowe) the upholsterer in Saint Bartholomew's, I saw the limbs of some of our new traytors set upon Aldersgate, which was a sad sight to see; and a bloody week this and the last have been, there being ten hanged, drawn, and quartered."

The gate gives the name to a City ward which was instituted in 1285, which is divided into two sections, each with four precincts. The first Alderman was William de Maiener; of the subsequent Aldermen, two have been baronets, Sir Samuel Garrard, Lord Mayor in 1709, whose ancestor, Sir William Garrard, was Lord Mayor in 1555, and whose great grandson, Sir John, was created baronet in 1621. Sir Samuel was the fourth in the baronetcy, and left issue two sons, both of whom succeeded, and both of whom died unmarried, the younger in 1767, when the baronetcy became extinct. The other was Sir John William Anderson, Lord Mayor in 1798, created baronet the same year, who died without issue in 1813, when the title expired. Three Aldermen also have been knighted, viz., Sir Peter Floyer, Sir Thos. Halifax, and Sir Peter Laurie. The Liberty of St. Martin's College was comprehended in the ward, but was exempt from its jurisdiction. Before the fire of 1666 there were six churches in the ward, those of St. John Zachary, St. Mary Staining, St. Olave, St. Leonard, St. Anne, and St. Botolph; of these the first five were consumed in the fire, and St. Anne's only rebuilt. St. Botolph escaped with a scorching. The most important religious establishment in the ward was the Collegiate Church of St. Martin's-le-Grand. Tradition says that it was founded in the time of the early British Christianity, by Wythered, King of Kent, in honour of Cadwallon, King of Britain. It was repaired and endowed *circa* 1056 by two brothers (Saxons), Ingelricus and Edward or Gerard, which was confirmed by William I., after the Conquest, by charter, wherein it is declared to be a Royal free chapel, with a collegiate establishment consisting of a dean and a fraternity of secular canons, with many privileges and immunities, including exemption from outward, civil, and ecclesiastical jurisdiction, and the right of sanctuary within the limits of the liberty.

Ingelricus was the first dean, and after him several distinguished men held the office, of whom William de Wykeham, the famous architect, Bishop of Winchester and builder of Windsor Castle, rebuilt considerable portions of the College; and James Stanley, brother of the Earl of Derby, who was instituted in 1493, and is supposed to have been the last.

The college with all its appurtenances was given by Henry VII., in 1502, to the Abbot and Convent of Westminster, for the performance of certain religious ceremonials; and on the suppression of the abbey, 34 Henry VIII., was transferred to the newly-created dean and chapter. It was suppressed finally in 1548, 2 Edward VI., and the same year, as Stow informs us, "the church was pulled down, and in the east part thereof a large wine tavern was builded, and withall down to the west and throughout the whole of the precinct of the college, many other houses were builded and highly priced, letten to strangers borne and others such as then claymed benefitte of privileges grannted to the canons serving God day and night (for so be the words of the charter of William the Conqueror) which may hardly be wrested to artificers, buyers and sellers, otherwise than as mentioned in the 21st of St. Matthew's Gospel."

The curfew bell was rung nightly, at eight o'clock, from the churchtower. Edward I. issued a proclamation that "in consequence of the many mischiefs, murders, robberies, and beating down persons by certain Hectors walking arm in arm, none should be so hardy as to be found wandering in the streets after the curfew had sounded at St. Martin's-le-Grand. The other churches where the curfew bell was rung in the City were St. Mary-le-Bow, St. Giles, Cripplegate, and Allhallows Barking. At the sound of the bell the great gates of Aldersgate were closed, but the wickets left open, which were also shut and fastened as soon as it ceased ringing, and were not opened again until the morning excepting by a special order from the Lord Mayor.

In digging the foundations for the Post Office in 1818, a range of Saxon or early Norman vaults were discovered, which had belonged to the college, the remains of a crypt of the time of Henry III., and a stone coffin.

St. Botolph's church, situated on the western side of Aldersgate Street, near Little Britain, is dedicated to a Cornish monk, who is said to have lived in the time of King Lucius, and was buried at Boston (Botolph's town), in Lincolnshire. It is an ancient rectory, formerly in the gift of the dean and canons of St. Martin, and was given along with the college to the Abbot and Convent of Westminster, and at the dissolution to the Bishop of Westminster, who was suppressed by Queen Mary, and the convent restored, to whom it reverted. Queen Elizabeth restored it to the new dean and chapter, who still hold it, subject to the approval of the Bishop and Archdeacon of London. It escaped the fire of 1666, became ruinous, and was patched and repaired at divers times until 1790, when it was rebuilt, a portion of the old church being retained in the eastern wall. It cannot be considered a handsome church exteriorly, but the interior is effective, although of mixed styles. It has a painted window of Christ's agony in the garden, executed in the dark age of glass painting. In another window, by Jas. Pierson, the figure of St. Peter is very fine. Having been spared by the Fire, the church contains a great many monuments of the old citizens of the fifteenth and sixteenth centuries. There is one to Daniel Wray, F.R.S., Deputy Teller of the Exchequer, who died in 1783, æt. 83. He was a learned man, and collected a large library of old authors, which his widow presented to the Charter House. Another, a tablet and bust, by Roubiliac, is erected to the memory of Elizabeth Smith, who died in 1750, æt. 15. There is an inscription commencing—

"Not far remote lies a lamented fair,
Whom Heaven had fashioned with peculiar care," etc.

At the north-east corner of Little Britain stood an alien Cluniac Priory, or Hospital, founded in 1377, which was suppressed with other alien houses by Henry V., and the endowments given to the parishioners of St. Botolph's, who founded a brotherhood of the Holy Trinity, in connection with the church, to celebrate masses in the church. It was suppressed *temp.* Edward VI., and the hall of the priory converted into a vestry and school. There were also two brotherhoods of St. Fabian and St. Sebastian, and a sisterhood of St. Katherine in the church.

St. Anne's Church is also called the Church of St. Anne and St. Agnes, from a tradition that it was built by two sisters so named, and in old records is styled St. Anne in the Willows, from its standing in a grove of those trees. The date of its foundation is not known, but a John de Chambrey was collated to the living in 1322. The rectory was under the patronage of the Dean and Canons of St. Martin's, and went with the college to Westminster. It was destroyed by fire in 1548, restored in 1624, again burnt in 1666, rebuilt by Wren in 1680, when the parish of St. John Zachary was united to it, and again "repaired and beautified" in 1701-3. Within its walls was buried William Gregory, Mayor of London 1451, in a chantry which he had founded. There was a monument to Peter Helwood, who was stabbed in Westminster Hall, in 1640, by John James, a Dominican friar, for his zealous prosecution of the Papists, as a justice of the peace. The inscription says :—

> "Reader, if not a Papist bred,
> Upon such ashes lightly tread."

The Rev. James Penn, lecturer at the church, was, along with the Rev. S. Aldrich, rector of St. John's, Clerkenwell, appointed to investigate the mystery of the Cock Lane Ghost.

There have been several notable Nonconformist chapels in and about Aldersgate Street. Early in the reign of Charles II., the Society of Friends established a meeting in Bull and Mouth Street, and George Fox frequently preached there. As was common at that time, the congregation was subjected to barbarous persecution. In 1662 a mob assembled, dragged them out into the street, beating and mauling them severely, and killing one outright.

In 1760 the meeting was given up, and the room taken by a congregation of Sandemanians from Glovers' Hall, who held it many years until they removed to Paul's Abbey Barbican. In 1767 appeared "A Plain and Full Account of the Christian Practices Observed by the Church in St. Martin's-le-Grand, etc.," which was attributed to the Rev. John Bernard, minister of the chapel, a learned man, and author of some other works, who was eventually expelled from his pulpit for "not being sufficiently humble, and for thinking too highly of his preaching abilities." He died in 1805.

Trinity Hall, at the corner of Little Britain, was occupied by a congregation of Nonjurors, and afterwards by a society of Moravians. It was here that a memorable event took place, which had an important influence in the great revival of religion in the last century, and resulted, along with other predisposing causes, in the outgrowth of the now large and influential sect of Wesleyan Methodists. John Wesley, in his journal, May 24th, 1738, writes: " In the evening I went very unwillingly to a society in Aldersgate Street, where one was reading Luther's Preface to the Romans. About a quarter before nine, while he was describing the changes which God makes in the heart through faith in Christ, I felt my heart strangely warmed. I felt I did trust in Christ alone for salvation; and an assurance was given me that He had taken away my sins—even *mine*—and saved *me* from the law of sin and death."

Hare Court Independent Chapel was built on ground leased for 999 years, from Sir Henry Ashurst, in the year of the Revolution, 1688. Originally it stood with an open space in front, facing Aldersgate Street, with a single entrance therefrom. It was built by a society gathered together in the reign of Charles II. by the Rev. Geo. Cockayn, who had been ejected from St. Pancras, Soper Lane, in 1662, consisting of many of the foremost citizens and several officers of the army. It was rebuilt in 1772, with three galleries, and a new entrance from Paul's Alley. In 1857, the chapel was disposed of, and out of the proceeds a new one built in Canonbury, to which was given the time honoured name of Hare Court, and which maintains the popularity of its predecessor.

In 1804 a congregation of Calvinistic Methodists assembled in a large room of Shaftesbury House, under the pastorate of the Rev. T. Madden, who removed hither with his flock from Bartholomew Close.

From the time of the Plantagenets to that of the Stuarts, Aldersgate Street was the Belgravia of London, the place of residence of prelates and nobles. Compared with other streets of the City, it was spacious and open, lined with magnificent buildings, and adorned with clusters and lines of ancient trees. Howell, in his *Londinopolis*, 1657, speaks of it as resembling a street in an Italian city; and Malcolm, in his *Londinium Redivivum*, 1805, says; " Aldersgate Street is very unequal in its buildings, but the majority are of superior excellence, and the various shops and warehouses of the first respectability. In width it is superior to most of the streets within the walls of the City."

The only one of the famous old mansions recently remaining was Shaftesbury or Thanet House. It was built by Inigo Jones for the Tuftons, Earls of Thanet, and was purchased by Anthony Ashley Cooper, Earl of Shaftesbury, the Achitophel of Dryden. Pennant says: " It was hired or purchased by the incendiary statesman, Lord Shaftesbury, for the purpose of living in the City to inflame the minds of the citizens, among whom he used to boast he could raise 10,000 brisk boys by the holding up of his finger. He attempted to get into the magistracy, but being disappointed in his views and terrified at the apprehension of the detection of a conspiracy he had entered into against his prince, he fled, in 1683, into Holland, where he soon died of the gout, heightened by rage and frustrated ambition."

The house was afterwards let for manufacturing purposes; in 1750 it became a Lying-in-Hospital, which was removed to the City Road, when it was opened as a Dispensary, with a Dissenting Chapel, called Shaftesbury Chapel, on the first floor, until the migration of the congregation to a new chapel opposite Westmoreland Buildings, called Aldersgate Chapel.

Petre, Dorchester, or London House stood on the west side of the street nearly opposite Shaftesbury House. It is supposed to have been built by Sir William Petre, who became rich by monastic plunder at the dissolution of monasteries, and died in 1572. It was occupied by his descendants until 1639, when it came into possession of Henry Pierrepoint, Marquis of Dorchester. During the Commonwealth it was made use of as a state prison, and after the Great Fire of 1666 had destroyed the palace of the Bishop of London, in St. Paul's Churchyard, became the episcopal residence of the see, many alterations being made, and the chapel built by various bishops, and was held by them until 1725. In 1748 it was occupied by Jacob Ilive, "the crazy printer and fanatical writer," and twenty years after by Seddon, the eminent cabinetmaker, ancestors of the Seddons of Gray's Inn Road, who had the misfortune to have it burnt, with the whole of his uninsured stock, on two occasions. Afterwards, also, Miss Seddon was burnt to death in the house, by her clothes catching fire.

The two mighty and illustrious northern families of Percy and Nevil had both of them a town mansion in Aldersgate Street on the western side—Northumberland House, on the site of Bull and Mouth Street; and Westmoreland House, on the site of Westmoreland Court, extending to Bartholomew Close. On the death of Henry, first Earl of Northumberland, at the Battle of Bramham Moor, 1408, and his subsequent attainder, King Henry IV. gave Northumberland House to Queen Joan for a wardrobe. Afterwards it became a printing office, then a tavern, and finally was divided into shops and tenements. Lauderdale House stood on the east side, a little north of Shaftesbury House. It was the residence of the Earl of Lauderdale, a member of the "Cabal" ministry of Charles II. Upon the site was built Bote and Walsh's distillery. Close by Shaftesbury House stood Bacon House, the residence of Sir Nicholas Bacon, Lord Keeper to Queen Elizabeth, and father of Lord Chancellor Bacon, one of the greatest of our philosophers. Ralph Montagu, third Baron and first Duke of Montagu, "as arrant a knave as any in his time," as Swift observed when he was raised to a dukedom, lived in Aldersgate Street until he built Montagu House, Bloomsbury (the British

Museum), when he removed thither. Charles Mordaunt, third Earl of Peterborough, one of the foremost men of the court of Queen Anne, was also a resident. On the west side of the street there is a picturesque old house (now a newsagent's shop) with an inscription stating that "This was Shakespeare's House," which may possibly be true, but there does not appear to be any documentary evidence in proof thereof. Mary, Countess of Pembroke, sister of Sir P. Sydney, the subject of Ben Jonson's famous epitaph, which was not inscribed on her tomb, died at her house in the street in 1621.

Many other distinguished personages have been born, lived, or died in Aldersgate Street, amongst whom may be noticed Milton, who in 1641 was living in a house at the bottom of Lamb (now Maidenhead) Court; Brian Walton, Bishop of Chester, the learned editor of the first English Polyglot Bible; Thos. Flatman, the poet, who was born in the street in 1657; the brothers Rawlinson, who resided in London House—Thomas, the "Tom Folio" of the *Tatler*, No. 158, and Richard, LL.D., F.R.S., and F.S.A., both antiquaries and great collectors of books. The Right Hon. Thos. Harley, a memorable member of the Corporation, and M.P. for the City, also resided here.

The Company of Cooks had their hall on the western side of Aldersgate Street, adjoining Little Britain. The company was incorporated by Letters Patent in 1480, by Edward IV., under the style and title of "The Masters and Governors and Commonalty of the Mystery of Cooks in London," and their charter was confirmed by Elizabeth and James I. with "a master, four wardens, and 25 assistants." The hall escaped the fire of 1666, but was destroyed by fire in 1771, and was not rebuilt.

There have been and still are many taverns and hostelries of considerable note in Aldersgate Street and St. Martin's-le-Grand. The most interesting is the "Mourning Bush," a very ancient tavern with a carved ivy bush for its sign—a timber-gabled house—with portions of the old wall of London for its foundations. It stood on the east side of the street, and had a back entrance in St. Anne's Lane. The landlord, during the time of the Civil War, was a devoted royalist, and on the execution of King Charles had the courage to paint his ivy bush black, and call it the "Mourning Bush." In 1749, the sign was changed to "The Fountain," and is referred to by Tom Brown as one of the "four or five topping taverns of the City," whose owners might look for an alderman's gown. In 1830, it was repaired and refitted, and instead of restoring the old historically interesting name, it has since been christened "The Lord Raglan." "The Bull and Mouth" (a corruption of Boulogne Mouth, or Harbour) a very ancient hostelry, originally standing in Bull and Mouth and Angel streets, with a galleried and gabled court-yard, now taken down. It was rebuilt in 1830, and to meet the more fastidious taste of the time its somewhat vulgar name was changed to the more euphonious "Queen's Hotel." On a stone tablet was the following inscription :—

> "Milo the Cretonian
> An ox slew with his fist,
> And ate it up at one meal,
> Ye gods, what a glorious twist!"

The new branch of the Post Office is being built on the site. Two doors from Barbican stood the "Bell," an inn worthy of being remembered as having been the resort of John Taylor, the Water Poet. The Albion is celebrated for its public dinners, and for the trade sales of London publishers. The Castle and Falcon is also a famous and very old inn, standing close by, and probably on a portion of the site of the gate.

Aldersgate Street has been the scene of some incendiary fires for the sake of plunder. Pepys, in his *Diary*, July, 1687, refers to a case in which two boys, one " a son of Lady Montagu's, I know not what Lady Montagu—got into the company of some rogues, who persuaded them to rob their fathers' houses of plate and other valuables, of which they appropriated the greater portion, and afterwards to set fire to a house in the street, that they might abscond with the goods that were thrown into the streets." Again in May, 1790, some scoundrels fired a house at the corner of Long Lane, which eventuated in the destruction of all the houses to Catherine (? Carthusian Street), involving the loss of property amounting to £40,000, that they might plunder them in the confusion. One John Flindall was apprehended, tried, and sentenced to transportation for robbery during the fire, when he offered to turn king's evidence, was accepted, and he revealed the diabolical plot, implicating especially two accomplices, Lowe and Jobbins, the ringleaders, who were hanged in front of the ruins. The Corporation took advantage of the clearance to widen Aldersgate in this part of the street, which had previously been very narrow, at a cost of £4,035.

The 7th of May, in the year 1603, was a day long remembered by the worthy citizens of Aldersgate Street, as that on which King James VI. of Scotland, entered the City through their gate to assume the title of James the First of England. The street was adorned with triumphal arches; arras and costly hangings decorated the fronts of the houses, and numberless banners and pennons floated in the breeze from the windows and points of the gables; the windows were filled with the beauty of the City—matrons and maidens; while the 'prentices and other venturous spirits perched themselves on the roofs, and the roadway below was densely crowded by citizens, who ever and anon made the welkin ring by their shouts of welcome. Sheriff Swinnerton, with ten followers in rich liveries, met the King at Waltham, and congratulated him on his safe arrival. At Stamford Hill he was met by the Lord Mayor Lee and the aldermen, all in scarlet robes, and 500 of the most eminent of the citizens, on horseback, all sumptuously apparelled in velvet, with gold chains round their necks. The procession passed slowly along, pausing at intervals to look upon some ingeniously-contrived pageant, and listen to the congratulations of the characters represented, and along Aldersgate Street to the Charter House, where the king was magnificently entertained by Lord Howard four days. In the evening the street was brilliantly illuminated by means of bonfires, cresset-bearers marching up and down, and lights from the windows.

In the last and the preceding centuries Little Britain was the great centre of the publishing and book-selling trades, and in Aldersgate Street, of which it is a tributary, there have lived several eminent members thereof. John Day, the famous printer, *temp.* Edward VI. and Elizabeth, occupied rooms over the gate. He printed a folio edition of the Bible, 1549, dedicated to King Edward VI.; published also the works of Ascham, Tindal, etc., and it was at his suggestion that Foxe wrote his *Book of Martyrs*, respecting which it was said—

> "He set a fox to write how martyrs runne,
> By death to lyfe."

Jacob Ilive, an eccentric printer, set up his press in London House, where he printed several of his own fantastic writings, such as "The speech of Mr. J. L., to his brothers, the Master Printers, on the Utility of Printing, 1730; etc., etc. Robert Chiswell, who died in 1711, of whom Dunton, in his *Life and Errors*, says, " The most eminent in his profession in the three kingdoms, I take to be Mr. Robert Chiswell, who well deserves the title of Metropolitan Bookseller of England, if not of all the world." John Hereford, whose last publication was the Newe Testament, 1548; Nicholas Borman; Anthony Scholcker, *viz* 1548, afterwards of Ipswich; William Tilly, who published the new Testament in 4to. in 1549: Henry Denham, at the sign of the Bear and Ragged Staff, Thomas Easte, at the sign of the Black Horse, and Thos. Whitchurch, at the sign of the Well and Two Buckets, St. Martin's-le-Grand.

Old Broad Street.

THE ward to which this street gives its name is unquestionably the richest in the City of London, containing within its limits, extending from Cornhill Ward on the south to Bishopsgate Ward on the north, and from Bishopsgate Ward on the east to Coleman Street Ward on the west, some of the most wealthy and important commercial establishments of the metropolis. Within its boundaries are the Bank of England, and a multitude of other high-class banks, the Royal Exchange, the Stock Exchange, several Insurance offices, Consulates, the South Sea House, the Inland Revenue Office, Drapers' Hall, Merchant Taylors' Hall, Carpenters' Hall, and an infinite number of merchants' offices, where mercantile transactions of incalculable magnitude take place daily. It comprehends within its area several of the most important commercial and financial streets of the City—Threadneedle Street, Lothbury, Throgmorton Street, Great Winchester Street, Princes Street, Moorgate Street,

Austin Friars, with other smaller streets, courts, and alleys, all full of life, bustle, and active commercial life. It comprehends six parishes— those of Allhallows-on-the-Wall, St. Martin Outwich, St. Bene't Fink, St Bartholemew-by-the-Exchange, St. Peter-le-Poor, and St. Christopher, Threadneedle Street. Besides these are the Dutch Church, of the Austin Friars, and the Walloon or French Protestant Church in Threadneedle Street.

Old Broad Street is a wide spacious thoroughfare extending from the end of Throgmorton Street to London Wall and Wormwood Street, whence it is continued northward to Liverpool Street by New Broad Street; at the south end, by Throgmorton Street, it diverges at a slight angle to the end of Threadneedle Street, this portion having formerly been called Little Broad Street.

In the time of Charles I. it was one of the most fashionable streets in London, the place of residence of several aristocratic families, including, amongst others, those of the Earls of Shrewsbury, the Careys, Barons Hunsdon, and Earls of Dover, and the Westons, Barons Weston, and Earls of Portland, extinct 1688. The most important house, however, was Winchester House, which, with its gardens, occupied the site of Great and Little Winchester streets. The mansion was built by Sir William Paulet, first Marquis of Winchester, one of the foremost men of his age, and a remarkable man in many respects. He was born in the year 1475, and lived to the age of 97, holding various offices of state during two-thirds of that period, and at his death left upwards of a hundred descendants. In 1539 he was created, by patent, Baron St. John of Basing, to which title, by writ of summons, 1299, he was eldest co-heir. In 1549 he was created Earl of Wiltshire, and in 1551 Marquis of Winchester. He was Comptroller of the Household to Henry VIII., an executor of his will, and guardian of the young king, Edward VI., and afterwards became Lord Treasurer, and was made Knight of the Garter. He died in 1572, having witnessed all the changes of religion, and the turmoils and troubles attendant thereupon. On being asked how he managed to maintain his position, and an unbroken flow of prosperity, amid all the religious and political fluctuations of his time, he replied that "he was made of the pliable willow, not of the stubborn oak." He was twice married, first to Elizabeth, daughter of Sir William Capel, Lord Mayor of London, who was mother of his heir, the second marquis. At the dissolution of the Augustine Friary, the house and grounds were granted by Henry VIII. to Lord St. John, who pulled down a portion of the friary, built a mansion which he made his town residence, and laid out the grounds afresh which extended to the City wall, with a footway across, leading to Moorgate. This footpath had gates at each end, which were kept locked during the night, and no one allowed to pass along it. The Marquis was also the builder of Basing House, Wiltshire, memorable for the siege it sustained in the subsequent civil war.

In modern times Sir Astley Cooper, the celebrated surgeon, resided in Broad Street, in a house at the corner of the paved court leading to St. Botolph's Church, Bishopsgate Street, where he held a morning *levée* of City patients. His fees, the first year he commenced, amounted to five guineas, and it was not until the 5th that they reached £100 and the 9th, £1,000. After that they rose rapidly to £1,500, and one year he received the sum of £21,000. Afterwards he removed to the West-End, but he found a sensible diminution of his receipts from those derived from the City millionaires. The abbot of St. Alban's also had his town house opposite St. Augustine's Gate. Even in the time of the Romans, this part of the City would appear to have been inhabited by the aristocratical section of the community, as in 1854 a magnificent tesselated floor, 28-feet square, was discovered, such as must have belonged to a large and high-class house. Humphrey de Bohun, Earl of Hereford and Essex, in 1243, founded on a plot of land extending westward from Broad Street, a priory for begging Friars of the order of St. Augustine, which flourished until the dissolution, when the house and grounds were granted to Lord St. John and the church, appropriated by King Edward VI., in 1551, to "John Alasco, and a congregation of Germans and other strangers fled hither for the sake of religion," the church to be called "the temple of the Lord Jesus," and in the hands of the Germans, or rather Dutch it still remains.

There is but one church in the street—St. Peter's, originally St. Peter the Apostle, but now St. Peter-the-Poor, a mean edifice, with an ungainly tower, and might well be designated "the poor" from its poverty of architectural merit. Maitland says that it "received the appellation from the mean condition (as is supposed) of the parish in ancient times. If so that epithet may at present be justly changed to that of rich, because of the great number of merchants and other persons of distinction inhabiting there." The probability seems to be that it derived that name from its proximity to the house of Begging Friars, who made a merit of their poverty, and this came to be called St. Peter by the Poor Friars, to distinguish it from St. Peter's, Cornhill, and others of the name. We have no knowledge of when or by whom it was built, but it is a very ancient foundation, as there is documentary evidence showing it to have been in existence in 1181. Among the rectors of St. Peter's have been some notable men. Richard Holdsworth, D.D., educated at St. John's, Cambridge, where he won a name for proficiency in arts and theology, became master of Emanuel College, and vice-chancellor of the university, who was preferred to the rectory in 1636. He was a zealous loyalist, and ejected from his living in 1642, his house plundered, and he imprisoned in the Tower. In 1645, he was nominated to the deanery of Worcester and elected Bishop of Bristol, but declined the dignity. He was permitted to attend King Charles at Hampton Court and Carisbrook Castle, but he suffered much by deprivation, sequestration, and several imprisonments. He died in 1649, and was buried in the church of St. Peter. Benjamin Hoadley, D.D., afterwards successively Bishop of Bangor, Hereford, Salisbury, and Winchester, who held the living from 1704 to 1720. He was eminent as a controversialist, and held views which would now be termed Rationalistic, approaching closely to Unitarianism, which were developed especially in his *Plain Account of the Sacrament,* and his *Discourses on the Terms of Acceptance.* When Bishop of Bangor, he published a sermon on "The True Nature of the Kingdom that Christ came upon Earth to Establish," from the text, "My kingdom is not of this world," which gave rise to the celebrated and long-protracted "Bangorian Controversy." He published a multitude of works, chiefly of a controversial character, and died in 1761.

John Scott, D.D., 1677-91, afterwards rector

of St. Giles-in-the-Fields, and canon of Windsor, a learned divine, author of *Cases of Conscience*, 1683; *Texts Cited by the Papists Examined*, 1688; *The Christian Life*, 1683; ninth edition, 1702; and other works, which passed through successive editions, and some translated into foreign languages. His entire works were published in two vols., fol., in 1718, and in six vols., 8vo., in 1826.

In the fifteenth century Venice held the secret and the monopoly of glass making. The works were situated on the island of Murano, and many attempts were made by other nations to learn the secret, but the Venetians asserted and spread abroad the report that it was impossible to make glass elsewhere equal to that of Murano, even with the same materials, the same workmen, and the same method of working, as there was something in the air of the island which imparted a lucidity and lustre, rendering the glass of the island superior to anything that could be produced in any other part of the world.

About the middle of the sixteenth century the manufacture was introduced into England, and works established in the Savoy and Crutched Friars. Early in the following century a company of noblemen and courtiers, with Sir Robert Mansell at their head, formed an association for the manufacture of glass, and built works for that purpose in Broad Street, near Austin Friars. At that time it was not deemed derogatory to the dignity of a nobleman to engage in the glass trade. In Venice the manufacture was held in such high esteem that those engaged in the profession ranked as gentlemen, and in France a decree was issued that glass-working should not lessen the dignity of a noble.

In 1615 the company employed as their manager or steward James Howell, afterwards Historiographer Royal to Charles II., whom they sent abroad to obtain information for the improvement of their processes, and to employ skilful workmen. He obtained from the Lords of Council a warrant to travel for three years, on condition that he did not visit Rome or St. Omer, and he started off in 1619, returning in 1621.

He tempted the best workmen, by a promise of a high rate of wages, especially Signor Antonio Miotti, from Lealand, who had been a master manufacturer, and was reckoned the ablest workman in Christendom, and from

Venice "two of the best gentlemen workmen that ever blew crystal."

Howell was a remarkable man, and led a somewhat varied life of vicissitude. After his continental tour he threw up his situation, not being able to bear the heat of the glass works, was elected a fellow of his college, and in 1626 became secretary to the council of the North, at York, and the next year was elected to represent Richmond, Yorkshire, in Parliament. In 1632 he went to Denmark as secretary to a special embassy, and on his return went to Ireland to seek employment under Wentworth, but failed in consequence of the recall and execution of that nobleman. In 1640 he obtained a clerkship in the council at Whitehall, but lost it on the breaking out of the Civil War, and in 1643 was committed to the Fleet for his loyal predilections, where he remained until the death of the king. On his release he found himself not only penniless, but in debt. He contrived, however, to maintain himself during the Protectorate by writing for the press, and at the restoration was appointed Historiographer Royal, which office he held until his death in 1666.

When Monk came to London to effect the

restoration of monarchy, he halted with his army in Finsbury Fields, had a conference with the Lord Mayor and aldermen, who coincided with him in his views, which were professedly the maintenance of a free Parliament. He quartered his men in the Broad Street Glass House, and passed himself into the City, amid the acclamations of the people, to the Bull's Head, Cheapside, where he took up his quarters. The glass works, despite the monopoly, was not a success, the manufacture was discontinued, and the house, or a portion of it, taken by the Pinmakers' Company.

The Pinmakers, or Pinners as they were usually called, were neither a numerous or a rich company. Indeed, Stow says that they met in Plasterers' Hall originally, and in his time the house had gone to decay, as "they were not worth a pin." The company was formed in the reign of James I., and was incorporated 2nd Charles I. (1636). The arms presented a a crowned half figure of Queen Elizabeth, with the motto, "Virginitas et unitas nostra fraternitas." Towards the end of the 17th century they held their quarterly courts of assistants in Cutler's Hall, Cloak Lane, Dowgate.

In the Guildhall Library is preserved the minute-book of the quarterly meetings from 1698 to 1723, some portions of which are engrossed. It commences with a list of members in 1698; then gives the minutes of the meetings in succession. The chief business appears to have been fining the members of the court 1s. for being late, binding and unloosing apprentices, and voting donations to the widows of members. The company has now entirely disappeared.

St. Augustine's passed through some strange mutations before it finally disappeared. Originally the home of a fraternity of begging friars, it became the stables and outhouses of the mansion of a nobleman. Then it was converted into a glass factory; a soldiers' barracks for a short time; after which it was appropriated by a City company, and finally became a great centre of Protestant Dissent, from whose pulpit were enunciated principles of theology at which, in the olden time, friars would have stood aghast. In the reign of Charles II., Anthony Palmer, who had been ejected from Bourton-on-the-Water, and who suffered much under the Act of Uniformity, an able and learned man, author of *The Tempestuous Soul calmed by Jesus Christ*, and other esteemed works, collected a congregation here, took a lease of the building, and fitted it up with two tiers of galleries, and died in 1678. He was followed by a long succession of ministers who preached Calvinistic doctrines, amongst the more notable of whom were George Townes, M.A., who had been apprehended in the pulpit at Bristol on a charge of having being implicated in the "Presbyterian Plot," was removed by *habeas corpus* to King's Bench Prison, and eventually acquitted. He suffered much persecution, and died of the stone, aggravated by his imprisonment, in 1685. Richard Wavel, famous for his pulpit oratory, who died in 1707. Joseph Hunt, D.D., a learned divine, who occupied the pulpit 37 years. He is highly panegyrised by Dr. Lardner for his erudition, strength of mind, and wonderful memory. Joseph Foster, D.D., born 1697, pastor of Pinners' Hall Church 1774-1753, author of *The Usefulness, Truth, and Excellency of the Christian Revelation*, written in reply to *Christianity as Old as Creation*. He was buried in Bunhill Fields. Caleb Fleming, D.D., born at Nottingham, 1698; pastor, 1753-1778, having been previously minister of a congregation in

Bartholomew Close. Author of a multitude of pamphlets—some published anonymously—quaint and obscure in style. He held opinions verging on Socinianism, and "set down as fools all who held different opinions," including Watts, Bradbury, Pike, Wesley, Whitefield, and Sherlock. This congregation only occupied the chapel in the mornings, and at the expiration of the lease, in 1778, the church was dispersed. In the afternoons an Independent Church, commenced by Thomas Cole, who died in 1697, rented the chapel. He was followed by Dr. John Singleton, who in 1704 removed with the church to Lorimer's Hall.

In that year (1704) Dr. Isaac Watts preached here in the afternoons until 1708, when he removed to the new meeting house in Duke's Place.

Then followed, in 1708, a congregation under the oversight of James Maisters, who came hither from Joiners' Hall, who, with his successor Thomas Richardson, removed in 1723 to Devonshire Square. About 1741 Mr. Weatherley's congregation of General Baptists came here from Artillery Place, Spitalfields, and continued until the expiration of the lease, when they removed to Berry Street. A sect of Seventh Day Baptists also occupied the chapel on Saturdays, under the pastorate of Thomas Bampfield, "who died a martyr in Newgate in 1684." The church afterwards removed to Curriers' Hall.

In 1779 a lease was taken of the chapel by Anthony Cole, a seceder from the Countess of Huntingdon's connection, who gathered together a numerous congregation, who assembled here until the expiration of the lease in 1799, when they removed to Founders' Hall.

Shortly after this the building was taken down, and all traces of it are now obliterated.

But that which rendered Pinners' Hall so conspicuous and celebrated in the annals of Nonconformity was the establishment of the Merchants' Lecture within its walls. In 1672, the Dutch war commenced, and Charles II. and his advisers, thinking it desirable that there should be peace at home in the religious world whilst there was war abroad, issued the memorable Declaration of Indulgence, in the preamble to which it was stated, "that there was very little fruit of all those forcible methods which had been used for seducing erring and dissenting persons, etc. His Majesty therefore, by virtue of his supreme power in matters ecclesiastical, took upon him to suspend all penal laws about them, declaring that he would grant a convenient number of public meeting places to men of all sects that did not conform, provided they took out licences, etc." This was welcomed by the Dissenters generally as a gracious act of toleration, but there were those amongst them who looked upon it as a stepping-stone to the re-introduction of Popery. Taking advantage of the indulgence, the Presbyterians and Independents who agreed in the fundamental principles of the Reformation, and in a desire to tear away from the Anglican Church the shreds of Popery which still adhered to it, met together, under the patronage of the merchants of London, and agreed to establish in Pinners' Hall a weekly lecture, to be preached on Tuesday mornings.

At first four Presbyterian and two Independent ministers, the most eminent of their day, were appointed to preach in turn. They were Drs. Bates, Manton, and Owen, and Messrs. Baxter, Collins, and Jenkyn, and for a time the lectures were continued with success and acceptance, and with tolerable unanimity, despite some little bickering on the questions of Predestination and Reprobation, occasioned by a sermon preached by Baxter, who defended his sermon in a tract entitled *An Appeal to the Light*, when Dr. Manton came forward and partially suppressed the clamour, but Baxter seceded.

A succession of distinguished ministers continued the lecture until 1694, when the Calvinistic question again cropped up, arising out of the reprinting of the works of Dr. Tobias Crisp, which were published under the editorship of his son in 1690, and written against by Mr. Williams, one of the lecturers. Discord sprung up, and an attempt was made to exclude him from the lectureship, upon which four of the lecturers,—Dr. Bates, and Messrs. Williams, Howe, and Alsop,—sent in their resignations, and set up an opposition lecture at Salters' Hall, at the same day and hour.

At the expiration of the lease the lecture was removed to Little St. Helen's, and afterwards to the chapel in New Broad Street, about 1780, but was very thinly attended.

The Independent Chapel in New Broad Street, to which the Merchants' lecture migrated, was built in 1728, for Dr. Guyse and a congregation who separated with him from Miles Lane. Dr. Guyse was a learned man and Merchant lecturer at Pinners' Hall, and was author of *A Paraphrase on the New Testament,* 1739, a voluminous and valuable work, as well as of some other works.

He was followed by John Stafford, D.D., who died in 1800, and was buried in Bunhill-fields; author of *The Scripture Doctrine of Sin and Grace, Twenty-five Sermons on the Seventh Chapter Romans,* etc.

A writer in Knight's *London* says: "If a stranger from any part of England, Scotland, or Ireland, however remote, were to pause in the midst of Broad Street, and enquire to what purpose that large pile of buildings opposite to him were appropriated, he would, ten to one, on learning that it was the Excise Office, have a livelier idea of the operations of the Board of Revenue, which has its seat there, than the inhabitant of London, provided that neither had been brought into direct contact with its officers by the nature of his business." In 1626, King Charles I. attempted to introduce the excise, but a unanimous vote of the Houses of Parliament compelled him to renounce the scheme. Nevertheless, in 1643, Parliament itself levied an excise, for the maintenance of the forces raised by them; the first articles on which the duty was laid were ale, beer, cider, and perry. The Commissioners of Excise sat in Haberdashers' Hall. An account of its establishment was given by Prynne, in a tract published in 1654, entitled, "A Declaration and Protestation against the Illegal and Detestable and oft-contemned New Tax and Extortion of Excise in General, and for Hops, a native and uncertain commodity in particular." An excise office was built in Smithfield, which was burnt down by the populace, and many riots took place in London in opposition to the tax, especially when salt and meat and other of the common necessaries of life were subjected to it; and a multitude of pamphlets, some of a very scurrilous character, appeared in opposition to it. The Excise office was afterwards removed to the mansion of Sir J. Frederick, in Ironmonger Lane, and remained there until 1768, when the trustees of the Gresham estates let the ground on which Gresham College and Almshouses stood, extending from Bishopsgate Street to Broad Street, to Government for £500 per annum, the City and Mercers' Company further agreeing to pay out of the Gresham funds the sum of £1,800 towards the demolition of the college and the building of the Excise Office. The architect was the elder Dance, who erected a plain but spacious and commanding looking brick building, which served the purpose of the commissioners until 1848. when the office was removed to Somerset House.

That portion of the grounds of the Gresham estate which faced Broad Street, was occupied by the almshouses founded by Sir Thomas Gresham in 1575, and bequeathed by him in trust to the Lord Mayor and Commonalty of the City of London. They consisted of eight tenements for eight poor men, with an annual allowance of £6 13s. 4d. and a load of coals, and a new gown every two years. On their demolition to make room for the Excise Office, they were removed to the City green-yard, in Whitecross Street.

Another Government office which stood in Broad Street was the Pay Office for the Navy. It was situated in a portion of Winchester House at the north-west corner of Great Winchester Street, has since been removed, and is now located in Somerset House.

The South Sea House formerly extended from Threadneedle Street to Broad Street, with a frontage in both streets; now it is confined to the former street in a more modern building. The company was incorporated in 1710 by Queen Anne, for the purpose of paying off a sum of ten millions due to the seamen who had been engaged in the French wars. In 1720 they obtained an Act of Parliament giving them a monopoly of trading to the South Seas. By a series of iniquitous frauds and deceptions they raised the shares to a fictitious value of 1,000 per cent., and caused the nation to fall into a sort of financial madness in their eagerness to get shares, which resulted in the "South Sea Bubble." The panic on its bursting caused the ruin of innumerable families, whilst a few clever rogues realised large fortunes. The company has long ceased to be a trading body, and the remnant of the stock, converted into annuity stock, is managed by Government, under the provisions of an Act of Parliament passed in 1753.

The district northward of Old Broad Street was formerly called Petty France, on which New Broad Street has been built. Seymoor in his edition of Stow writes: "Petty France; the greatest part of this is new built, and called New Broad Street. It is a most regular building; the houses are after the manner of those by Hanover

Square and Burlington Gardens, and are the most elegant buildings in the City."

In New Broad Street, besides the Independent Chapel, mentioned *supra*, a Presbyterian chapel was erected in 1729, for a congregation which removed hither from Hand Alley, Bishopsgate, where a Church had been formed early in the reign of Charles II. by Thomas Vincent, who rendered himself famous by his labours amongst the sick during the Plague. Dr. John Evans, a pious and eminent man, was minister of the Church at the time of the removal, and was author of a great number of published sermons, and other works, including "Two sermons preached at the opening of a new meeting place, in New Broad Street, Petty France, December 14th and 21st, 1730." John Allen, M.D., was a subsequent minister of the chapel, author of several sermons which were printed; and another was John Palmer, a controversial writer, and opponent of Dr. Priestley. At the expiration of the lease in 1780 the chapel was taken down and the church dispersed.

An illustration of the primitive mode of stopping the ravages of fire occurred in 1314, when permission was asked by the officials of

Broad Street ward to cut down an elm tree standing by London Wall and sell it, to enable them to purchase a new cord for their "wardhoke," a hook which was kept in each ward of the City for the purpose of pulling down houses to prevent the spreading of fires.

In 1500 an inquisition was held to ascertain the liability of the ward to maintain two bridges over the Wall Brook running from "Vynesbury," now broken, and to replace the hinges of Bishopsgate, when it was found that the Prior of Holy Trinity was bound by his charter to keep one of the bridges in repair, and the Prior of the New Hospital without Bishopsgate and Broad Street ward the other jointly, and that it devolved on the Bishop of London to maintain the hinges of the gate, as he claimed a stick from every load of wood that passed through the gateway.

Broad Street of late years has become a thoroughfare of immense traffic, especially in the mornings and evenings, of cabs and pedestrians going from and to the half-dozen railways which have erected stations and termini in Liverpool Street, so much so as to render it at certain times of the day one of the most thronged streets of the City.

Chaucer and the Tabard.

THE Tabard has passed away! Another of the relics of old London—a link between the picturesque past and the prosaic present—rich as it was in remembrances associated with the birthtime of English poetry, is now a thing of the past. We have but few of these relics of Bygone London remaining; it is true the Tower, St. John's Gate, and the house of Sir John Crosby still linger with us; but who knows how soon the site of the Tower will be wanted for a railway station, the gateway of the old knights be found to be an obstruction in the way of Pickford's vans, and the old Bishopsgate Street house swept away by the broom of "improvement?"

If there be one spot within the bounds of London that may be especially termed classic—which may be looked upon as sacred to poetry—that spot is Southwark, despite its hop warehouses, in the midst of which stood the Tabard. The legend of the ferryman's daughter and the foundation of the monastery and church of St. Mary Overies is redolent of romance. In Clink Street, Shakespeare lived and wrote, and in the theatre on Bankside he gave utterance to his inspired imaginings; in St. Saviour's Church sleeps Gower, the contemporary of Chaucer; and in one grave repose Fletcher and Massinger; whilst on Bankside, in twin fraternity, dwelt Beaumont and Fletcher.

More than to others should this spot and the Tabard be dear to the citizens of London, for he to whose shrine pilgrims of the hostelry were wending their way was the son of a London merchant; and he who describes, and has rendered immortal, that riding to Canterbury, in April of the year of grace, 1383, was born within the walls of the City.

The Tabard owed its origin to the Abbey of Newere Mynstre, Winchester, which was founded by King Alfred, and afterwards removed outside the walls, when it assumed the name of Hyde Abbey, *temp.* Henry I. Alwyn, the eighth abbot, was uncle to King Harold, and fought, with twelve of his monks, under his standard at Hastings. In process of time the Abbey waxed rich, and in 1307 the Abbot purchased a plot of land near the palace of the

Bishop of Winchester, and thereon, as Stow informs us, "built a faire house for him and his train when he came to the City to Parliament." At this spot was a convergence of roads from the southern and western counties, from whence started eastward "The Pilgrim's Road" to Canterbury, in consequence of which the Abbot built, in close contiguity, a hostelry for the reception of pilgrims, where they might repose until a sufficient number was gathered together to proceed in company for protection from the dangers of the road. It was built in the picturesque style of the period, with gables to the street, cross timberings and latticed windows; in the interior was a large courtyard, with balustraded galleries running round it, leading to dormitories; and there was a "Pilgrims' Hall," a large room some 45 feet in length, with open fireplaces and long tables, at which the pilgrims dined and supped during their sojourn. At the dissolution, 1538, it was sold, along with the Abbot's House, and is described as "The Tabard of the Monastery of Hyde, and the Abbot's place, with the stables and gardens belonging thereunto." Still, however, it retained its character of an inn, and in the reign of Elizabeth was repaired and partially rebuilt by "Master J. Preston." A view of it, as it then appeared, is given in Urry's edition of Chaucer, 1721, representing it in the old timbered and gabled style, with a beam stretching across the road, from which the swinging and creaking sign was pendant, and on which was an inscription,— "This is the Inn where Sir Jeffry Chaucer and the nine-and-twenty pilgrims lay on their journey to Canterbury, anno 1383." In 1673, in pursuance of an Act of Parliament, this cross beam, with its supporting posts, was taken down, but the inscription, after the rebuilding, was painted over the gateway, where it remained until 1813, when it was erased.

The street front of the inn was consumed in the great fire of Southwark, 1676, along with 600 other houses, but was immediately rebuilt, presumably in facsimile of the original, with its courtyard, galleries, pilgrims' hall, and quaint old sleeping-rooms, and it is possible that some parts which escaped the fire may have been a portion of the Tabard, where Chaucer sat as "a chiel takin' notes," and where the pretty prioress, the wife of Bath, the knight and the squire, and the Sumpnour and the Pardoner chatted and laughed and flirted; certainly the courtyard was the identical spot where the merry party mounted their nags and palfreys, to ride forth along the "Pilgrims' Road" to St. Thomas's shrine. The pilgrims' room was divided into three apartments; on its walls was formerly a fragment of tapestry, representing a procession of pilgrims, which afterwards disappeared. After the fire, says Aubrey, "the ignorant landlord or tenant, instead of the ancient sign, put up the Talbot or Dog." Truly he must have been ignorant or destitute of veneration for antiquity or poetical feeling, to commit such an act of vandalism, and his successors cannot have been much better not to have restored the old time-honoured designation.

For all time will the name of Harry Bailly, the jovial landlord of the Tabard towards the end of the fourteenth and beginning of the fifteenth centuries, be remembered. He was a notable burgess of Southwark, and evidently a popular character; he is supposed to be identical with Henry Tite Morton, who, in 1380, was assessed, with his wife Christiana, at 2s. to a subsidy, rented the customs of the borough in fee farm at £10 per annum; was bailiff to Southwark, whence his appellation, Henry le Bailly; represented the borough in the Parliament of Westminster, 50 Edward III., and in that of Gloucester 2 Richard II. A jolly fellow he seems to have been, well adapted for his profession:—

> "A seemly man our hoste was withall
> For to have been a Marshal in a Hall;
> A large man he was, with eyen steep,
> A fairer burgess is there none in Chepe:
> Bold of his speech and wise and well ytaught,
> And of manhood, him lacked righte naught;
> Eke thereto was he right a merry man
> And spake of mirth amonges ot'thing
> When than we hadden made our reckonings."

It was in the merry spring time of the year 1383, as the inscription on the sign informs us—

> "Whenne that April with his showres sote
> The drought of March, hath pierced to the rote,
> And bathed every vein in such licour
> Of which virtue engendered is the flower,"

a time of the year when

> "Longer folk to go on pilgrimage,
> And specially from every shire's end
> Of Englande, to Canterbury they wend,
> The holy, blissful martyr for to seek,
> That them hath holpen, when that they were sick,"

that Chaucer and his company met at the Tabard.

St. Thomas of Canterbury was murdered in the year 1170, by four knights, instigated thereto by a passionate exclamation of King Henry II., who was at feud with him relative to the respective rights of Monarchy and the church, and his shrine during the intervening years had become one of the most popular in the kingdom; the Saxon people, down-trodden by their Norman lords, looking upon him as a sort of clerical Robin Hood, the defender of the rights of the poor against Regal and Baronial oppression, and in process of time it had become resplendant with precious metals and gems, the offerings of pious devotees. Says Chaucer—

> "Befell that in that season, on a day,
> In Southwark, at the Tabard, as I lay,
> Ready to wenden on my pilgrimage
> To Canterbury, with devout courage,
> At night was come unto that hostelry;
> With nine and twenty in a company,
> Of sundry folk by aventure yfall
> In fellowship, and pilgrims were they all,
> That toward Canterbury wouldeh ride.
> The stables and the chambers weren wide
> And well we weren eased atte best" (well accommodated).

He then gives a series of photographs of the pilgrims, representatives of various classes of the people of England at a most eventful period of our history—a period when Wycliffe was laying the foundations of the Protestant Church; when

Wat Tyler and his fellow serfs were rising in assertion of their liberties; when Chaucer and Gower were fashioning the English language into shape, as contradistinguished from the Norman-French of the Court; when the feeble Richard occupied the throne, to be shortly driven hence by his cousin Bolingbroke, which eventually led to the Wars of the Roses, and resulted in the extinction of a vast number of the Norman families, rendering it easier for the Saxon element of the kingdom afterwards to gain the ascendancy.

Amongst the company are a knight, a worthy man, who had done deeds of prowess in all parts of the world, yet was meek as a maid, who was dressed in a "fustian gipon, alle besmattered" with marks of travel; along with him was his son, "a younge squire, a lover and lusty bachelor," with "lockes curl'd, as they were laid in press;" also his attendant, a yeoman "clad in green," and under his belt "a sheaf of peacock arrows bright and keen."

There was also a prioress

> "That of her smiling was full simple and coy;
> Whose greatest oath n'as of Saint Eloy,"

who sung the service "entuned in her nose full

sweetly, and French she spoke full fair and fetisly, after the school of Stratford-atte-Bow."

> "A monk there was, an outsider, that loved venery;
> Of pricking and of hunting for the hare,
> Was all his lust for no cost would he spare."

"A friar there was, a wanton and merry Limitour (a licensed beggar), a full solemne man, who

> Was an easy man to give penance

There as he wist (to those he knew) to have a good pittance." Who

> "Knew well the taverns in every town,
> And every hosleter and gay tapstere,
> Better than a lazar or a beggere."

A merchant with a forked beard, "a Flandrish beaver hat, and bootes clasped fair and fetisly."

A threadbare clerk of Oxenford, on a horse as "lean as a rake," who would rather have twenty bookes of Aristotle and his philosophy,

> "Then robes rich, fiddle, or psaltry."

A sergeant-at-law, "wary and wise, that often had been at the Porvis" (the portico of St. Paul's, where lawyers met for consultation).

A Frankelin, with white beard and sanguine complexion, and a silken "Gipciere" (purse) hanging from his girdle; a pompous sort of man, fond of good living, in whose house "snowed meat and drink, who was an important man in his county, lord and sire at sessions, high sheriff, and full often knight of the shire."

A haberdasher, a carpenter, a webbe (weaver), a dyer, and a tapiser; citizens with pouches full of silver; "yclothed in one livery of a solemn and great fraternity."

> "Well seemed each of them a fair burgess,
> To sitte in a Guildhall, on the dais,"

and all fitted by wisdom to be aldermen.

With them had they a cook, "to boil the chickens and the marrow bones," who, perhaps in consequence of the hot nature of his vocation, had a wondrous *penchant* for "draughts of London ale."

A shipman, "who rode upon a rouncy (hack) as best he could," somewhat after the style of modern mariners.

A doctor of physic, "well grounded in astronomy," who

> "Kept his patient a full great deal
> In houres by his magic natural."

A wife of Bath, who had had five husbands and was ready for a sixth; a buxom dame, dressed in scarlet hosen and hat as broad as a buckler, who smirked and smiled upon the squire, much as the widow Wadman did, in an after age, upon Uncle Toby.

A poore parson, "rich of holy thought and work," a learned man and clerk "that Christe's Gospel woulde preach living at home in his parish instead of running up to London," unto St. Paul's, to seek for a chantry for souls.

"For Christe's love and his Apostles twelve,
He taught, but first he followed it himselve."

With whom was his brother, a ploughman, "that had of dung laid many of fother: a true swinker, who would thresh and dike and delve for Christ's sake, for every poore wight, withouten hire, if it lay in his might."

A miller, "a stout carle for the nones, full big of brawn and eke of bones, with beard red as any sow or fox, a wart on the cop of his nose, whence sprouted a crop of heres, red as the bristles of a sowe's ears; a jangler and goliardeis (reveller), who could well stealen corn and tollen thrice," and moreover "a baggepipe well could he blow and soun, and there withal he brought us out of town."

A Manciple, or purchaser of victuals for Inns of Court.

A Reeve, or land steward, a slender, choleric

man, closely shaven and shorn, with calfless legs, who "ever rode hinderest of the rout."

A Sumpnour, or appositor of an Ecclesiastical court, "with a fine red cherubinne's face and a visage with knobs on his cheeks, of which children were afraid; a great drinker and garlic eater, and likerous (lecherous) as a sparrow."

His friend, a Pardoner, fresh from Rome, with a wallet "bretful of pardons and relics," making more money of them in a day than the parson of the parish in "moneths tway."

When this motley company had settled their reckoning with Harry Bailly, their host, he offered to be their guide to Canterbury, and as this was not the time when pilgrims hobbled along with peas in their shoes, he suggested that, to beguile the tedium of the way, they should each tell a tale, one going and another returning, and that he who told the best, should, on their return to the Tabard, be entertained at supper at the cost of the rest, which proposition was carried by acclamation; and the following morning the merry party mounted their nags in the court-yard and set forth, headed by the landlord, beside whom rode the miller, playing lustily on his bag-pipes until they got clear of the town, when the tale-telling commenced.

It may be supposed that they arrived safely at Canterbury, knelt at the shrine of the martyr, purchased their brooches, in evidence of their having been there, and caroused again on their return in the Pilgrims' Hall; but Chaucer leaves them on the road, prevented, perhaps, by troubles or death from giving the tales of the backward journey.

As the pilgrimages are coming into fashion, it may be that fresh gatherings may take place in Southwark; but it will not be at the Tabard, under the guidance of Harry Bailly, but at the London Bridge terminus, under the leadership of Cook, the excursionist; and it is to be feared that, instead of a Chaucer to depict the humours of the journey, their proceedings will be narrated by a newspaper correspondent.

The Priory of the Holy Trinity, Aldgate.

NOT long had the Norman dynasty ruled over England. Scarcely more than a third of a century had elapsed since the Norman Duke unfurled his standard at Hastings, and in that interval the first William and the second William had passed away, and Henry le Beauclerk, by an act of usurpation had leapt into the vacant throne, which belonged by right to his elder brother Robert. The Saxon people, reft of their lands, deprived of their liberties, and subject to oppressive laws, had become the vassals and serfs of their Norman feudal lords, and chafed with sullen submission under the yoke. Great, therefore, was their delight when their new king announced his intention of marrying a daughter of their old line of kings—a descendant of the great Alfred, and they cherished hopes that by this infusion of Saxon blood into the veins of their future kings, the Saxon race would be elevated in position, and that, being vastly more numerous, they would eventually, by marriages, absorb the Norman few and England again become Saxon.

Matilda, Henry's Queen (born 1079, married 1100, died 1118), was the daughter of Malcolm Canmore, King of Scotland, by Margaret, daughter of Eadward, the Ætheling, who was the son of Eadmund Ironside, the lineal descendant of King Alfred. She was originally called Editha, which name was changed, at the request of her godfather, Prince Robert, brother of her future husband, who wished her to be named after his mother. "Matildem quœ prius dicta Edithe," say Ordericus Vitalis. In the year 1093, her father was slain before Alnwick Castle, and her mother died of grief shortly after. Donald Bane usurped the throne of his nephew, and Eadgar, the Ætheling, removed his nephews and nieces to England, not deeming them safe in Scotland. Matilda was educated in the Nunneries of Romsey and Wilton, under her aunt, Christina, the Abbess. She had two or three eligible offers of marriage, and it was with some reluctance, and not until a council had determined that she was under no religious vows, that she accepted the hand of the king.

She became very popular by influencing the

king in the reformation of abuses, the granting of charters of privileges, and making good laws. Robert of Gloucester says—

> "Many were the good laws that were made in England
> Through Maud, the good Queen, as I understand."

Amongst other good deeds besides founding the Priory, she established a hospital at St. Giles-in-the-Fields, built a bridge over the river Lea, afterwards called the bridge of Stratford-le-Bow, which was so named because it was the first "bowed" or arched bridge built in England, and was generally called Maud's Bridge; made new roads, repaired old ones, and was a benefactor to the Abbey of St. Alban's, in whose "Golden Book," now in the British Museum, is her miniature, with an inscription, "Queen Matilde's gave us Ballwick and Lilleburn."

William of Malmesbury thus sums up her character :—" She was singularly holy . . . a rival of her mother's piety; never committing any impropriety. Clad in hair cloth, beneath her royal habit, in Lent, she trod the thresholds of the churches, barefoot. Nor was she disgusted at washing the feet of the diseased." She had issue a son, William, drowned with his bride and a host of nobles in the " Blanche Nef," when coming from Normandy, and a daughter, afterwards the Empress Matilda, mother of King Henry Second.

The most splendid act of munificence on the part of the Queen was the foundation of the magnificent Priory of the Holy Trinity, in the year 1108, which became in process of time the greatest and richest priory in the City.

At this period, when the City was a forest of spires and towers, there stood, on the north-east of Leadenhall Street, just within Aldgate, four parish churches, those of St. Catherine, St. Michael, St. Mary Magdalene, and the Blessed Trinity. The church of St. Michael is supposed to have been one of the most ancient Christian temples in England; at this time the earth had risen twenty feet above its level, and it was only necessary to take down the tower to make way for the priory. The body or crypt of this venerable relic of antiquity was discovered a few years ago, and unhappily destroyed. The church erected to the honour of Christ and St. Mary Magdalene was founded by Siredus, charged with an annual payment of 30s. to the Dean and Chapter of Waltham, which the Queen compounded for by giving them possession of a mill.

These four churches and parishes were cleared away for the site of the priory, which was built on the ground occupied by that of St. Michael. It was 300 feet in length facing Leadenhall Street, and was bounded on the east by what is now the street of Houndsditch.

Just outside the gate was the church of St. Botolph the Briton, a rectory of very ancient date, belonging to and standing on the land of the Knighten Guild, which was given by the knights to the prior and brethren, who rebuilt it and placed their arms over the door. It was repaired 1661, escaped the fire, became ruinous, and was rebuilt 1741-4.

After the clearance of the land, the buildings rapidly rose, and, when completed, were filled with Canons Regular of the order of St. Augustine, with Norman as the Prior, and is said to have been the first House of Canons Regular established in England.

For endowment, the Queen granted to the fraternity lands within the walls, which, when they obtained the Soke outside the walls, was called "the Inner Soken," the boundaries of which are described in a book called *Dunthorne*, written by one of the brethren, as extending from

Aldgate to the Bailey of the Tower, to St. Olave's Church, Coleman Church, and Fen Church, by the house of Theobald Fitzloo, " the lane leading wherto is now stopped, because it had been suspected of thieves," then by the Church of St. Michael to Lime Street, and by the Church of St. Andrew as far as the Chapel of St. Augustine-upon-the-Wall. She gave them also Aldgate and £25 per annum from the city of Exeter.

Thus runs the deed of gift: "Maud, by the grace of God, Queen of England, to R. Bishop of London, and all the faithful of the Holy Church, greeting. Be it known to you that I, by the advice of Archbishop Anselm, and with the assent and confirmation of my Lord King Henry, have given and confirmed to the Church of Christ, seated near the walls of London, free and discharged from all subjection, as well to the Church of Waltham, and all other churches, except the church of St Paul, London, and the bishops, with all things appertaining to the same, for the honour of God, to the Canons regularly serving God in the same with Norman the Prior, for ever, for the redemption of souls, and of those of our parents. I have in like manner given them the gate of Aldgate, with the Soc belonging to the same, which was my lordship, and two-third parts of the revenue of the city of Exeter. And it is my will and I command that the said Canons hold the lands and all things belonging to the Church, well and peaceably and honourably and freely, with all the liberties and customs which my Lord, King Henry, by his charter confirmed to them, so that neither wrong nor injury be done to them. Witness: William, Bishop of Winchester; Roger, Bishop of Salisbury; Robert, Bishop of Lincoln."

Henry confirmed this deed, with further privileges of sac and soc, thol and theam, ingfang theft and outfang theft, and all other their customs, as were within as without.

The Inner Soke is identical with the present ward of Aldgate, but there is no record to show that the priory was represented in the Court of Aldermen for this ward, as they were afterwards for their Outer Soken.

Soon afterwards, in the year 1115, the Priory had a considerable accession of landed property, by a grant of what now constitutes the ward of Portsoken.

In the reign of King Eadgar, thirteen knights

who had done service to the realm, asked the king to bestow upon them a tract of land lying desolate outside Aldgate, comprising what is now covered by the Minories, Houndsditch, Petticoat Lane, etc., and Whitechapel to the Bars. Eadgar consented on two conditions, that they should each be victors in three combats, one under ground, one upon ground, and one above ground, and that on a certain day they should tilt with lances against all comers in East Smithfield. All this was accomplished by the knights with great glory, and the king made them a grant of the land, constituting them a guild under the name of the "Knighten Guild," the land being named "Portsoken," signifying the "Franchise at the Gate."

Eadgar's charter of incorporation was confirmed by Eadward the Confessor, William I., William II., and Henry I.

After the establishment of the priory, the knights of the guild, for the glory of God and the Blessed Trinity, and out of a chivalrous admiration of their pious Queen, gave to the prior and canons the whole of their land, franchise, and liberties, and the church of St. Botolph the Briton, and took upon themselves the habit of the order, becoming members of the fraternity.

In attestation of their grant they placed their charters upon the altar of the priory church, and gave Norman, the prior seisin of the land in the church of St. Botolph, which stood upon the land; Barnard, Prior of Dunstable; John, Prior of Derland; Geoffrey Clinton, Chamberlain of London, and other clerks and laymen being witnesses thereof. King Henry gave a confirmatory charter, as did, afterwards, Gilbert, William, and Roger, Bishops of London, St. Alphage, Archbishop of Canterbury, and Popes Alexander and Innocent, the latter adding that the Church of St. Botolph should be served by one of the canons of the priory, removable at the discretion of the prior.

In consequence of this acquisition, the prior was admitted as a Ward Alderman of the City of London, the land, although lying beyond the boundaries, being within the liberties of the City. He met in the Council Chamber, took part in the deliberations, feasted in the hall, and rode forth in pageants, clad in scarlet as other aldermen, but had his robes cut in clerical fashion.

Allen, in his History of London, intimates that he sat in the Guildhall, in a clerical capacity, to look after the interests of the church, which was not correct, his position there being the representative of the temporalities of the Ward.

Prior Norman appears to have been entrusted with the superintendence of the building of the priory, and, like others not trained in commercial pursuits, to have been somewhat unthrifty in the expenditure of money, for we find that when he had built up his refectory, kitchen, and larder, his funds were exhausted, and he had not the wherewithal to supply the necessary food for his hungry canons; but the matrons and maidens of the city passing by, and seeing the tables laid out without the necessary appliances, brought them loaves of bread every Sunday for the week's consumption, until the rents began to come in and they were able to provide for themselves.

After the destruction of the four churches it became necessary to celebrate mass in two parts of the new church at the same time, which caused a great deal of confusion and discord, until at length a separate church was built for the St. Catherine's parishioners in the priory churchyard, where mass was performed by one of the canons; but the people were required to attend the conventual church at festivals and fasts, and to have their children baptised there. This gave rise to some ill-feeling and disputes, the people wishing to have all the services and sacraments of religion celebrated in their own church; and in 1414, when William Haradon was prior, the matter was referred to the Bishop of London for arbitration, and he decreed that St. Catherine's should have a baptismal font, and be allowed to ring their bells on Easter day; that they should celebrate the feast of the dedication of their own church within its walls, but should attend at the festival of the dedication of the conventual church, and then and there "give their pence, halfpence, and farthings in token of submission;" and that the Sacrament in St. Catherine's Church should be administered by a canon of the Priory, "but that the Priory should be at no other charges for the chapel." All this the bishop, "out of his paternal affections, yielded unto."

The church was denominated St. Catherine Cree, the word Cree being an ancient method of spelling the name of Christ, as pronounced by the

French, and was added as being an adjunct of the conventual or Christ Church. A bell tower was built 1504, Lord Mayor Sir John Perceval having left money for that purpose. The present church was built 1630, and escaped the fire of 1666. It was at its dedication that Laud indulged in Popish ceremonials, which aroused the indignation of the Puritans, and assisted in paving the way of the Archbishop to the block. The churchyard of St. Catherine was a popular place for the performance of moralities and miracle plays, which took place on Sundays. There is an entry in the parish books—" Received of Hugh Grymes, for licence given to certain players to play their interludes in the churchyard from the feast of Easter An. D'ni. 1565, until the feast of St. Michael the Archangel, next coming, every holyday, to the use of the parish, 27s. 8d." Hans Holbein is supposed to have been buried in the church.

The Priory had not been built twenty years when it ran a great risk of being destroyed by the fire of 1136, second only to the great conflagration of 1666, which broke out near London stone, and destroyed the City westward to Clement's Danes, and eastward to Aldgate, the flames sweeping up to the walls of the Priory, northward to St. Paul's Cathedral, which was partially, or, as Matthew Paris states, entirely, consumed, and by London Bridge, which was of wood, and entirely burnt, into Southwark.

Ralph the Prior, *circa* 1145, with the consent of the Canons, exchanged a plot of land near the river, in the outer-soken, and "all the mills there in the shambles," with Maud, Stephen's queen, for land in Hertfordshire, where she built and endowed the Hospital of St. Katherine, which was repaired and enlarged by Queen Eleanor in 1273. It was removed to Regent's Park in the present century to make way for St. Katherine's Docks.

King Henry II. having debased the coin of the realm, Stephen, the Prior, 1180, demanded £25 12s. 6d. from the city of Exeter, as the then value of the £25 per annum granted out of the city revenues. The citizens refused to pay the additional 12s. 6d., but were compelled by a mandate from the King.

In the year 1215, when King John was at feud with his Barons, Matthew Paris informs us that, after the siege of Northampton, the Barons came, by way of Bedford and Ware, to London, entering the City by Aldgate, and that "as they passed along, they spoiled the Fryars' Houses and searched their coffers," on which occasion, doubtless, the Brethren of Holy Trinity, lying so near the gate, would have black-mail levied on them. At the same time they repaired the ruined gate and put it in a state of defence, obtaining the materials from the houses of the Jews.

Eustacius, the eighth Prior, 1264, appointed Theobald Fitz-James as his deputy in the Aldermanship, he deeming it inconsistent with his spiritual vocation to perform secular duties.

William Rising became Prior in 1377, when there is a record of his taking the oaths as Alderman.

The year 1348-9 (23rd Edward III.) was long after remembered for a great pestilence, which broke out in Northern Asia, spread over Europe, and this year committed terrible ravages in London. The city graveyards became choked with corpses, and suburban cemeteries were extemporised for the wholesale reception of the dead. Nicholas, then Prior, sold to John Grey, clerk of the Corporation, a plot of ground in the outer-soken, near East Smithfield, to be used as a place of burial, with the condition annexed that it should be called the Churchyard of the Holy Trinity, "which ground he (John Grey) caused, by the aid of divers devout citizens, to be enclosed with a wall of stone." It was consecrated by Ralph, Bishop of London, and a chapel built "for the honour of God," and near by King Edward built a small monastery " of our Lady of Grace," in gratitude for preservation from shipwreck in a tempest at sea.

One Sunday morning, the 11th of May, 1471, when the brethren were at Mass, they were alarmed by an attack on Aldgate. For some days arrows had been shot into the City over the wall, and the houses of the outside suburb had been burnt. The besiegers were Sir Thomas Nevil, usually called the Bastard of Fauconbridge, and his followers. He was a kinsman of the Great Earl of Warwick, who, after his defection from the cause of Edward IV., had made him Admiral of the Lancastrian fleet. Warwick had fallen a month ago at Barnet, and the Yorkist King Edward in consequence became firmly established on the throne, when Sir Thomas conceived the mad project of landing with his sailors, marching to London, and re-establishing the Lancastrian family. The Londoners shut their gates against him, but he broke down Aldgate on this Sunday morning, and several of the insurgents rushed through when the portcullis was let down, and those within were slain by the citizens, headed by Basset, Alderman of the ward. The Lieutenant of the Tower then came up with a body of troops, the portcullis was raised, and the Bastard and his followers driven into Essex, " with sharp shot and fierce fight," being pursued as far as Mile End.

The priory waxed rich, grew famous, and flourished during a period of 433 years, no doubt becoming luxurious, idle, and corrupt, like other fraternities; until at length, in 1531, the end came. King Henry VIII., wishing to reward Sir Thomas Audley, afterwards Lord Chancellor and first Baron Audley of Walden, for his service as Speaker, in the impeachment of Wolsey, cast his eye upon this Priory, sent for Nicholas Hancock, the last Prior, whom he cajoled with complimentary praises, commending his hospitality, and telling him that a man of his merit and ability deserved higher preferment, and that if he would surrender the Priory into his (the King's) hands, he should have something better. After some hesitation the Prior gave up the house, the Canons were sent to other houses of the same order, and the Priory, with all its appurtenances, bestowed on Audley.

Sir Thomas Audley determined to build himself a mansion on the site, and offered the church to any one who would take it down, but it was so strongly built that no one would undertake the cost. He then pulled it down himself, and allowed any one to have the materials who would carry them away, giving the four large bells to Stepney Church, and the five smaller to St. Stephen, Coleman Street. He then added new buildings, where he dwelt until his death, 1544, when the property passed, by the marriage of his daughter, to Thomas Howard, Duke of Norfolk, who was beheaded 1572, and it was then called Duke's Place. It descended to their son, Thomas Howard, Earl of Suffolk, who sold it to the Corporation, was eventually taken down, and streets built on the site. The only vestige remaining is a stone arch between 73, Leadenhall Street and 39, Mitre Court.

The Priory possessed a messuage, dovecote, and garden of seven acres, on the east side of

Houndsditch, which were given to Sir T. Audley, and which he bestowed on Magdalen College, Cambridge. In the street leading thereto, one of the priors had built some cottages for bedridden people, which Stow remembered as having seen in his boyhood, the bedridden people, men and women, lying by the windows, that devout persons might see them as they passed and bestow alms upon them: which street, afterwards, according to Munday, was inhabited by "these men, or rather monsters in the shape of men, who profess to live by lending, and yet will lend nothing but upon pawns."

Stow, who lived in the parish of St. Andrew Undershaft, and was buried in the parish church, speaks from personal recollection of the Prior "keeping a bountiful house for rich and poor, as well within the houses as to all comers at the gate," and, when a boy, of going to farmer Goodman, in the outer-soken, where Goodman's Fields now are, for milk at the rate of "three pints, hot from the kine, for a halfpenny."

The inhabitants of Duke's Place being left without a church, after the demolition of the Priory Church, attended that of St. Catherine Cree until the reign of James I., when Trinity

Christ Church was built for them out of the ruins of the Priory, and was consecrated in 1622. It escaped the Great Fire, and has since been called the Church of St. James, Duke's Place. In Strype's time it claimed the right of solemnizing marriages without licence or proclamation of banns.

Convent of the Sisters Minoresses of the Order of St. Clare, Aldgate.

WONDROUSLY different was Plantagenet London from that of the Victorian era: different in every respect, notably in size, population, and aspect. It was chiefly comprised within the walls, which commenced at the Postern Gate of the Tower, and completed the circuit at the river near the present Blackfriars Bridge. There were a few outlying groups of houses and villages; a road along the river strand through the little village of Charing to Westminster, and marshes on the north, with causeways to the villages of Clerkenwell, Hoxton, and Islington. It was, however, an eminently picturesque city, with its gabled and timbered houses, its monastic edifices, and its church towers. It was computed that then two-thirds of the entire space was occupied by religious edifices and their grounds. Towards the end of the fourteenth century there were within the walls, eight friaries, five priories, four nunneries, five collegiate establishments, seventeen hospitals with resident brotherhoods, nine other religious fraternities, and more than one hundred parish churches. At that time the court end of the town was the neighbourhood of the Tower. There royalty dwelt; and clustering round were the mansions of nobles and the town houses of bishops and abbots.

The locality immediately under notice was a road running from the Tower postern, outside the City wall and ditch, to Aldgate, along what is now called the Minories. Aldgate, or Ealdgate, so named from its antiquity, was the eastern outlet from the City, the great Essex road running eastward therefrom. Immediately within the gate stood the magnificent priory of the Holy Trinity, founded by Matilda, Queen of Henry I., and close by was the town house of the Barons Nevil, afterwards Earls of Westmoreland, who gave an abbess to the convent of St. Clare. Outside the gate there stretched an open expanse of country, with foliaged trees, meadows, and silver streamlets, where, on holidays, the young citizens gambolled, practised archery, and, in the more secluded parts, whispered in the ears of the young citizenesses " the old, old tale." Looking eastward, the low square-towered church of the village of Stebenhede (Stepney) by the riverside morasses might be seen; and nearer London, its chapel-of-ease, at the villa Beatæ Mariæ Matfelon, on the Essex road, whilst more to the north might be discerned the priory of St. Mary Spittal, founded a century previously. Here, outside the gate, in the year of grace 1293, Edmund, Earl of Lancaster, and Blanche, his countess, whilom Queen of Navarre, founded the convent of Minoresses of the order of St. Clare, dedicated to the " Blessed St. Mary," and amply endowed it with lands and messuages. St. Clare, Clara, Claire, or Chiara, as the name is rendered in different tongues, was born of a noble and wealthy family at Assisi, 1193, died 1253, and was canonized 1256. She was exceedingly beautiful, and had many offers of marriage, but when quite young, despite the opposition of her parents, resolved to dedicate herself to God. St. Francis had just then founded the Franciscan branch of the Mendicant Orders, and lived with ten " Frati Minores," in a hut on the Porziunculo, near Assisi, living austere lives, in absolute poverty, depending upon charity for their daily food, and maintaining strict silence, excepting when it was absolutely necessary to speak. To them Clare fled, and desired to be admitted as a nun of the order. She was followed by her kinsfolk, but clung with such tenacity to the altar, that they were compelled to leave her. She then founded the Order of Poor Clares, or Sisters Minoresses, with rules of the most rigid austerity, relating chiefly to abstinence, poverty, and silence. Their bed was the bare earth, they usually went barefooted, and were habited in grey robes, girdled with a knotted rope, and a white coif on the head. Within fifty years after her death, however, they were released from the vow of poverty, and the others were modified, from which time they accumulated property, built themselves comfortable houses, and indulged in social converse. The first convent was erected outside the walls of Assisi, but afterwards removed within, where a splendid church—the church of Santa Chiara d'Assisi—was erected over her tomb. In pictures St. Clare is usually represented either with the Pix, to denote piety, or the lily, the emblem of purity. She was generally spoken of by the nuns as the "Madre Serafico."

Edmund Plantagenet, surnamed Crouchback,

was the second son of King Henry III.; born 1245, died 1295. In his eighth year, 1253, he was created Earl of Chester, and invested by the Pope with the title of King of Sicily and Apulia, but neither was of much value, as the former was soon afterwards transferred to his elder brother Edward, afterwards King Edward I., and Conrad, the real King of Sicily, was still living. He was afterwards created Earl of Leicester, 1264, and Earl of Lancaster, 1267. He fought in the wars of Gascony, Wales, and Scotland, and was two years in Palestine. He had grants of the forfeited castles and manors of the rebel barons, Simon de Montfort, Ferrers, Earl of Derby, and Nicholas de Segrave, and had licence, 21 Edward I., to castellate his house, the Savoy, in the Strand. His death occurred in France; he had invested Bordeaux, and not being able to reduce it, grief brought on a disease which terminated fatally. His body was brought to England and buried in Westminster Abbey, but not until, in accordance with the instructions in his will, all his debts were paid. He marrried, first, Aveline, daughter and heiress of William de Fortibus, Lord of the Seigniory of Holderness, Co. York, who *d.s.p.* the following year.

Secondly, he married Blanche, daughter of Robert, Earl of Artois (third son of King Louis VIII., of France), and relict of Henry, King of Navarre, by whom he had issue Thomas, second Earl, who, after heading the rising of the barons against Gaveston, *temp.* Edward II., was taken prisoner at Boroughbridge, Co. York, beheaded at Pontefract, and attainted 1321. Henry, his brother, was restored in the earldoms, whose son Henry was created Duke of Lancaster, 1351, but *d.s.p.m.*, leaving issue Maude and Blanche, the latter of whom married John of Gaunt, Earl of Richmond, afterwards Duke of Lancaster, by whom she had issue Henry of Bolingbroke, afterwards King Henry IV.

Piously disposed, as we may charitably suppose them to have been, or perchance for the welfare of their souls—as it was usual, in that age, to make bargains with Heaven to build religious houses as the price of exemption from the pains of purgatory—the Earl and Countess built the nunnery in the precincts of the court, and filled it with nuns of the order of St. Clare, brought over from some Continental convent by Queen Blanche, "to serve God, the Blessed Virgin, and St. Francis," for which they had a licence from

King Henry III. Stow informs us that the frontage of the convent was fifteen perches twenty-seven feet in length, with all needful interior appliances, and garden land; doubtless a pleasant home for the Sisters, with its outlook over the Essex fields and the river Thames, with its quaintly-fashioned vessels passing up and down. It was well endowed by its founders, but had other benefactors as well, and had messuages in the Vintry, Wood Street, Lad Lane, Lombard Street, Christ Church Lane, Shirburgh Lane, etc. The Sisterhood also held the Manor of Apuldercome, and had a grant from William Walshe, 7 Edward IV., of a messuage, called Harteshorn, in the parish of St. Mary Matfelon.

The original licence for the foundation is dated 21 Edward I. A charter was granted to "the sisters Minoresses, without Aldgate," quitting them of tallage of their land in the City, dated 9 Edward II.; and in the fourteenth of the same reign, another to "the Abbey of the Minoresses of St. Mary of the order of St. Clare, without the walls of the City," confirming the holding of certain lands and messuages "gotten of divers well-affected persons." Other charters of confirmation were granted to the Sisterhood, 2 Henry IV., and 1, 16, 25 Henry V.

The Sisters of St. Clare flourished here for a period of 246 years, praying, fasting, and mortifying the flesh, with intervals possibly of laughing, feasting, and enjoyment of their pleasant home; or it may be, as we know is often the case, even with the Angelic sex, when thrown together for days and years, the fasting and feasting and prayer might be mixed up with ingredients of wrangling, envy, and jealousy, until it all came to an end, when the ruthless Tudor king laid his sacrilegious hands on the monastic establishments, and spared not even the homes of the gentler sex, and the house of the Sisters Minoresses was surrendered by Dame Elizabeth Salvage, 1539.

During these two-and-a-half centuries the Sisters witnessed many important events in the annals of England; the deposition and murder of kings Edward II. and Richard II., the usurpation of Henry VI. and Richard III., the Wars of the Roses, the rise of Lollardism, the Interdict of the Kingdom under John, the Reformation, the introduction of the press, and the birth of English literature under Chaucer and Gower. It may be that the prioress who rode to Canterbury with Chaucer's pilgrims was the head of the Aldgate Minoresses.

> "There was also a nun, a prioress,
> That of her smiling was full simple and coy;
> Her greatest oath was but by Saint Eloy;
> And she was cleped Madame Eglantine.
> Full well she sang the service divine,
> Entuned in her nose full sweetley;
> And French she spake full fair and fetisly,
> After the school of Stratford-atte-Bow."

From their own windows they would see many a gay cavalcade of barons, knights, and ladies issue from the portals of the Tower to follow the sport of hawking in the fields, or play at some martial or other game, and many a brilliant procession going forth to tournament in Smithfield, or coronation in Westminster. They would behold the coronation pageants and feasts in the Tower of Richard II., the marriage of the rival Roses in the persons of Henry VII. and the Princess Elizabeth, and that of Prince Arthur and Catherine of Arragon, when a splendid tournament was held hard by. Their soft hearts would also often be awakened to compassion at hearing of the bloody deeds perpetrated in their neighbourhood, the murder of the young princes by their uncle, Richard of Gloucester, and the decapitation of Lord Cobham, Bishop Fisher, Sir Thomas More, Queen Anne Boleyn, and many another noble and distinguished personage. From their lattices, too, they would look upon the riding forth of the barons of the realm through Aldgate to attend the Parliament of Edward I., 1299, held at the mansion of Lord Mayor Wallis, at Stepney; the Wat Tyler mob rushing along, "with shouts and cries as if all the devils of hell had come in their company," to ransack the Tower, chop off the heads of the Lord Chancellor and Treasurer, and rudely kiss the King's mother, the "Fair Maid of Kent," and Princess of Wales, in 1381; and again in 1450, that of the Jack Cade insurgents, when they took Lord Say and Sele from the Tower and beheaded him in Cheapside.

After the dissolution, the Priory became the residence of John Clerke, Bishop of Bath and Wells, 1523-41, Master of the Rolls, and Diplomatist, who was poisoned in Germany, when sent on an Embassy to the Duke of Cleves, to explain to him why Henry VIII. had divorced his sister; after whom it was inhabited by some officials of the Tower, and in 1552 was granted to

Henry Grey, Duke of Suffolk, by King Edward VI. Afterwards it became a storehouse for arms, and workshops for the fabrication of implements of warfare, but does not seem to have been of high repute, as Dryden says, "a comic writer who does not cause laughter, or a serious dramatist who does not excite emotion, is no more a good poet than is a Minories gunsmith a good workman."

The Abbey of St. Mary of Graces, or East Minster.

IT was in the autumn of the year 1347, that a storm-shattered vessel might be seen threading its way up the Thames. Its single broad sail was rent in divers places, its single mast broken, and considerable portions of its lofty poop and its high pointed stem reft away. It had come from Calais, and in mid-channel had encountered a terrific tempest, every soul on board deeming himself lost, and offering up heartfelt prayers to the Virgin or his favourite saint for succour, or for intercession in case of death. Nevertheless, like English mariners in every after, and indeed former age, the crew depended not on prayers alone, but battled manfully with the winds and the waves, and at length with great difficulty succeeded in getting their vessel into the river, and slowly ascended its reaches, with their rent sail fluttering in the still boisterous wind.

It was said of one our Norman monarchs, when

he desired to pass over into Normandy, whilst a storm was raging and the seamen represented the perilous nature of the attempt, "Who ever heard of a King being lost at sea? go I will, and at once, storm or no storm," and he did go, arriving safely at his destination. Perchance the fact of this Calais ship having a king aboard, with the immunity of kings from shipwreck, may have had something to do with its escape from destruction, at any rate it did survive the peril, and its having done so was the cause of the establishment of the Abbey of St. Mary of Graces.

The royal personage who passed through the peril of the Straits was none other than the victor of Creci and Calais, the illustrious Plantagenet, Edward the Third. The three sons of Philip IV. of France having successively died without issue, his nephew, Philip of Valois, according to the Salique law, became his successor, but Edward of England claimed the throne as son of the daughter of Philip IV., and entered France to assert his claim. He met his rival, Philip VI., at Creci, with 36,000 men, opposed to the French army of 130,000, and obtained a great victory, 36,000 of the French being slain and the rest taking to flight. He then marched

P

to Calais, which he invested and took after a most obstinate defence of twelve months, on August 4th 1347, after which occurred the famous historic incident of the six brave burghers of Calais presenting themselves before the victor in their shirts, and with ropes round their necks, as voluntary victims to sate the vengeance of the king and save their town, and their subsequent pardon at the intercession of the Queen. Notwithstanding the obstinate defence of the town, the King could scarcely do less than accede to Philippa's request, since within its walls she had presented him with a fair daughter, afterwards called Margaret of Calais.

His Queen and the newly-born princess were with him in the frail bark when it was tossed hither and thither, and its timbers riven by the storm, and in the midst thereof he prostrated himself and made a solemn vow, calling upon the nobles and ecclesiastics who accompanied him to bear witness thereto, that if God in His mercy should permit him to land safely in England, he would build and endow on the spot where he landed a monastery to the honour of God and our Lady of Graces.

At length, after beating up the river as well as

they were able with their broken rudder and shattered sails, the mariners drew the vessel alongside the shore a little to the east of East Smithfield, when the royal party landed, and passed, amid the acclamations of the few people congregated on the river bank, to the Tower, and offered up thanks in the chapel for their deliverance.

Very different in aspect was the district eastward of Aldgate and the Tower when King Edward and his retinue landed there, from what it presents at present, with its docks, wharves, and warehouses, its stately ships and steam-vessels, to which the ship of King Edward might have served as a boat slung on davits by their side; its wilderness of houses, countless miles of the squalid homes of wretchedness, poverty, and crime; with multitudes of lofty chimneys, belching forth volumes of black smoke rising from the midst, and railways traversing it in every direction, accompanied by the incessant thunder of rushing trains, and the screeching whistle of the locomotive.

The scene that presented itself to the monarch when stepping upon the river bank from his vessel was that of a flat expanse of pasture land

and marshes, stretching away northward and eastward, protected from inundation by the embankment of the river, the work of the Romans, which, however, was not always effectual, as the Thames frequently overflowed defective portions of the bank and laid the land under water. There were also many rills and streamlets meandering along from the high lands of the north, which lost themselves in the marshes or found an outlet into the river.

Scattered here and there on the more elevated parts were a few hamlets, mere clusterings of a few cottages, claybuilt, with cross timberings and straw-thatched roofs, with holes for chimneys, and in the walls latticed openings to admit light to the interiors. These were the abodes of cowherds, who tended their masters' cattle in the marshes, swineherds who drove their charges into the neighbouring forest to pick up the fallen acorns, fishermen who plied their daily toil on the river, and a few artizans, carpenters, smiths, and wrights, such as are now met with in remote country villages. These people were wretchedly poor, half-starved, ill-clad, and profoundly ignorant, the slaves of monkish superstition, and the downtrodden serfs of the nobles. Yet had they within them the old Saxon instinct of freedom and liberty, and they were the men who in the following reign ranged themselves under the banners of Wat Tyler and Jack Straw.

Westward stood the Tower of London, frowning grimly on the river bank—at once a palace, a fortress, and a prison. Stretching northward therefrom, was the eastern wall of the City terminating in Aldgate, whence ran the road into Essex. Within the gate, with its tower overtopping the wall, might be seen the magnificent Priory of the Holy Trinity, founded by Matilda, the Saxon Queen of Henry I., in the year 1108, and outside, along the road now called the minories, the humbler and more lowly built convent of the Nuns Minoresses of the Order of St. Clare, founded in 1239, by Edmund, Earl of Lancaster. And hard by, close to the gate, was the Church of St. Botolph, formerly belonging to the knights of the Cnighten guild, now to the Holy Trinity Priory. Close by the landing place was the hospital of St. Katherine, founded in 1148, by Matilda, Queen of Stephen, for the repose of the souls of her children—Baldwin and Matilda; refounded in 1273 by Eleanor, widow of King Henry III. Eastward was St. Chad's

Well, round which grew up a hamlet, so called, since corrupted to Shadwell. Further on lay the hamlet of Stebenhithe (Stepney), with its low broad-towered church. North-westward of it, in the Essex Road, was the chapel of St. Mary Matfellon, whose name has given rise to much discussion, without any satisfactory result. Afterwards it was called the White Chapel, and hence it gave the name to the line of road running from Aldgate. Northward might be discerned the priory and hospital of St. Mary Spittle, a timber building with an angle turret, founded by Walter Brune and his wife, in the year 1197; and not far distant, on the west, the priory of St. Helen, with its hall, hospital, cloisters, and crypt, founded in 1210 by William Fitz-William, and dedicated to the Holy Cross and St. Helen, mother of the Emperor Constantine.

Here, then, on the north side of St. Katherine's Hospital, and eastward of Little Tower Hill, King Edward laid the foundations of the monastery, and made it subject to the monastery of Beaulieu, in France, of which he was the founder. It was called also East Minster, or New Minster without the walls.

"In the charter of endowment, dated March

2nd, 1349, he gave the abbot and monks all those messuages, with the appurtenances at Tower Hill, which he had of John Corey, in pure and perpetual alms, ordering the house to be called 'The Royal Free Chapel of St. Mary of Graces.'"

In another charter it is said, "The king founded this house in remembrance and acknowledgement of the goodness of Almighty God, and of the Lord Jesus Christ, and of the Blessed Virgin Mary, whom he had often called upon and found helpful to him by sea and by land; in wars and other perils, and therefore ordered this house to be called 'The King's Free Chapel of the Blessed Virgin of Graces, *in memoriam Gratiarum.*'"

He imported some monks from Beaulieu to occupy the house, and appointed Walter de Sta Cruce first president of the chapel, "whom he enjoined kindly to receive and treat the said religious who were to profess religion in the said chapel."

The house was a stately building of the new decorated Gothic, with its floriated windows, crocketted pinacles, flying buttresses, and clustered pillars, presenting a fair aspect to passers by on the river, as it stood a little way back from the bank, glowing in its pristine freshness and beauty. And the boatmen would rest on their oars and listen to the matins or vespers chanted by the brethren within its walls.

In the 50th year of his reign, the King further augmented the endowment by placing the Manors of Poplar, of Gravesend, and other manors in Kent, in trust for the abbey.

Of the Abbots, the names of but few have survived. William de Santa Cruce, formerly Abbot of Geronden, was the first, to whom the king made an allowance of £20 per annum for the maintenance of the household.

William Warden, probably his successor, was Abbot in 1360. Paschalis occurs in a record of the eighth Henry V., 1418. John Langton is named, in 1495, in a bequest from Jane Hall, of a tenement for her soul's health. In 1494 he was presented to the vicarage of Gedington, and in 1498, by Sir T. Lovelace, to that of Stokedanbey in the diocese of Lincoln. John, probably the same, occurs in 1503. Henry More made his profession as Abbot in 1516.

The house was surrendered in 1539, when the

revenues were estimated at £602 12s. 6d. gross, and £546 10s. net per annum.

Dugdale says: "Of the manner of the surrender we find no account which gives occasion to guess that it was done by such as were in no authority, and therefore it was thought fit to conceal the knowledge thereof. It was granted by Henry VIII., 34th, to Sir Arthur D'Arcy; was clean pulled down, and of late times, in place thereof, is built a large storehouse for victuals, and convenient ovens are built there for baking biskets for the Royal Navy, and it is the victualling office for the same to this day. The grounds adjoyning, and belonging formerley to the said abbey, have small tenements built thereon."

Maitland, 1772, in his *History of London*, says that a portion of the original building was then standing, "now converted into a bisket bakehouse," which is probably an error, as Dugdale states that it was "clean pulled down."

In the Chapter House, Westminster, there is an impression of the seal of the abbey, appended to an indenture for the foundation of Henry VII.'s Chapel. In the centre is the Virgin with the infant Jesus, with a royal personage—probably Edward III.—kneeling in prayer on the dexter side, and a group of figures on the left. Underneath is a shield of the Royal arms, and the legend, SIGIL LUM COMVNE MONASTERIJ BEATE MARIE DE GRACIIS.

The Barons Fitzwalter of Baynard's Castle.

IT was with mutterings of discontent and gloomy forebodings that Saxon London beheld, soon after the victory at Hastings, the erection of a fortress at the east end of their city—replaced soon after by the earliest portion of the present Tower of London—and two huge castles to the west, ostensibly to guard, really to keep the City in awe. Duke William, after the Battle of Hastings, knowing how important it was to hold possession of the largest and most influential city in the kingdom, hastened up to London. The citizens, who felt not disposed to surrender their liberty to a foreigner, and who, influenced by Archbishop Stigand, had caused Eadgar the Atheling to be proclaimed king, crossed the river to oppose his advance but were repulsed; nevertheless, the Conqueror did not follow up his success by entering London, but burnt Southwark and went to subjugate the western counties. During his absence, the citizens deeming it the best policy to submit, at any rate for the present, tendered their homage to him at Berkhamstead. Suspicious, however, of their loyalty, he caused the castles to be erected, and to conciliate the citizens granted them a charter of four and a half lines written in Saxon, on a piece of parchment six and a half inches long and one broad. This laconic charter ran thus:— "William the King salutes, with friendly greeting, William the Bishop, and Godfrey the Portreve, and all the burgesses within London, both French and English, and I declare that I grant you to be all law-worthy as you were in the days of King Edward; and I grant that every child shall be his father's heir, after his father's days; and I will not suffer any person to do you wrong. God keep you."

The two western castles were built, at the confluence of the Fleet with the Thames. The one by the Baron Montfichet, soon afterwards destroyed by fire, stood at the bottom of Addle Hill, where the Carron Wharf is now located, and its western walls were washed by the Fleet, whose course was afterwards diverted further westward to make a site for the Dominican Friary.

It was built by the Norman, Ralph Baynard, feudal baron of Little Dunmow, Essex, who had followed the Conqueror to England, and was rewarded for his services at Hastings with grants of land in Essex and Middlesex, and, in connection with Baynard's Castle, the military governorship of London, as castellan and standard-bearer of the City.

William, third lord, sided with Helias, Earl of Maine, in his attempt to throw off his allegiance to King Henry I., for which he was attainted, and his estates and honours given to Robert Fitz Richard, fifth son of Richard de Tonbridge, descended by the bend sinister from the Dukes of Normandy.

The church of St. Andrew, on the east side of Puddle-dock Hill, is supposed to have been built by Ralph Baynard, and was called "St. Andrew juxta Baynard Castle" until the erection, near by, of the King's Wardrobe, when it came to be called "St. Andrew by the Wardrobe." It was repaired by the parishioners in 1627, destroyed in the Great Fire of 1666, and rebuilt in 1672. The advowson was held by the Fitzwalters, and after passing through various hands came to the Crown in 1633.

This Robert was steward and cupbearer to King Henry I., and a great favourite with that monarch, who, upon the attainder of William Baynard, bestowed upon him his forfeited estates, including the barony of Dunmow, and the castle by the Thames, with its appurtenant civic offices. He took an active part with Longchamp, Bishop of Ely, against the designs of John, Earl of Moreton, upon the crown, during the absence of his brother, Richard I., in Palestine; died in 1198, and was buried at Dunmow. Robert Fitzwalter, his eldest son, died in 1234.

The tyranny of King John caused great discontent amongst the barons, with whom Fitzwalter agreed in sentiment, and this discontent was brought to a head, driving the barons to take up arms, by a flagrant attempt on the honour of Fitzwalter's family. Matilde, "the fair," his daughter was exceedingly beautiful, and John attempted her chastity, which she indignantly repelled; "whereupon," says Stow, "and for other causes of the like sort, there ensued a war throughout the realm. The barons being received into London did great damage to the king; but in the end the king did not only banish the said Fitzwalter, among others, out of the realm, but also caused his castle and other houses to be demolished. After that a messenger was sent to Matilda the Fair about the king's suit, but she not consenting to it, was poisoned." This was done at Dunmow, by sprinkling a deadly poison on a poached egg, which she ate.

Her exiled father retired to France, and entered into the service of the king. In the year 1214, John of England invaded France, and concluded a truce with the French for five years. The two armies lying on each side of a river one day, soon after the signing of the treaty, an English knight of great strength and valour came forth and challenged any French knight to a joust, when Fitzwalter crossed the river in acceptance thereof, and at the first course unhorsed his antagonist in gallant style. "By God's truth," exclaimed John, "he is a king indeed who is followed by such a knight as that!" "He is your own knight, O king," said one of his attendants, "Robert Fitzwalter whom you banished." Upon this the king sent for him to his tent, restored him to favour, gave him back his estates, and granted him permission to repair his castle and houses.

The tyranny of the king, however, compelled

the barons again to take up arms, to establish on a sure basis the laws and liberties granted by Edward the Confessor, of whom Fitzwalter became the head by the title of "Marshal of the Army of God and of the Church." Eventually they obtained the reluctant signature of the Magna Charta at Runnymede, when Fitzwalter was one of the twenty-five barons appointed to enforce the observance of the charter. In the reign of Henry III. he fought with great bravery under the baronial banner at the Battle of Lincoln, where he was taken prisoner, but was not detained long, as the next year he went as a crusader to the Holy Land, and displayed great valour at the siege of Damietta.

Camden informs us that he instituted the custom of the flitch of bacon of Dunmow. He says: "On the Priory here" (Dunmow), "Robert Fitzwalter (a powerful baron in the time of Henry the Third) instituted a custom that whoever did not repent of his marriage, nor quarrelled with his wife within a year and a day, should go to Dunmow and have a gamon of bacon. But the party was to swear to the truth of it, kneeling upon two hard pointed stones set in the Priory churchyard for the purpose, before the prior, the convent, and the whole town."

Sir Robert, Kt., his grandson, was summoned to Parliament by writ, 23rd Edward I. (1295) and died in 1325. In 1275 he alienated Baynard's Castle, by licence, to Robert Kilwardby, Archbishop of Canterbury, who removed hither the Dominican or Black Friars from Holborn, but took special care to reserve all the rights and official duties connected with his barony.

In the year 1303, before Sir J. Blount, Kt., Lord Mayor, a specification of his duties to the City was drawn out, which he swore upon the Evangelists to observe, and to the utmost of his power to maintain the rights and liberties of the citizens. His privileges and immunities in connection therewith are also given, which were confirmed by Sir John on the part of the Corporation. As this document presents some curious features of London life in the beginning of the 14th century, it is given below *in extenso*.

The Rights that belonged to Robert Fitzwalter, Chastilion and Banner-Bearer of London and Lord of Wodeham.

"The said Robert and his heirs ought to be

and are chief Banner-bearers of London in and for the Castlry which he and his ancestors have of Baynard's Castle in the said City. In time of war the said Robert and his heirs ought to serve the City in manner hereinafter written.

"That the said Robert ought to come upon his Horse of Service, with 20 men at arms, mounted, harnessed with mail or iron, even to the great door of the Minster of St. Paul, with a Banner of his Arms displayed before him. And when he has thus come, then ought the Lord Mayor of London, with the Sheriffs and Aldermen, come on foot out of the Minster to the said door, with his banner in his hand, and the banner ought to be gules, an image of St. Paul d'or, the feet, hands, and head, argent, with a sword argent, in the hand of the said Image.

"And as soon as they shall have come forth, the said Robert shall alight from his horse and salute the Mayor, as his companion, saying, 'Sir Mayor, I am come to do my Service which I owe to the City,' and the Mayor shall answer, 'We allow you here as our Banner-Bearer, this banner of the City to carry and govern to your power, to the honour and profit of our City.' Then shall the said Robert take the banner in his hand, and the Mayor, Aldermen, and Sheriffs shall present him with a horse of £20 value, with a saddle, garnished with the arms of the said Robert, and covered with a sendal of the same arms, and deliver £20 to his Chamberlain for the charges of the day.

"The said Robert shall then mount the horse, banner in hand, and desire the Mayor, forthwith, to cause a Marshall to be chosen out of the host of London, which being done, he shall then cause the signal to be sounded through the City, for the commons to assemble, and follow the banner carried by the said Robert to Aldgate, and a Council of two sage persons from each ward be chosen, in the Priory of the Holy Trinity, to look to the safe keeping of the City in case the said Robert should have to absent himself for the purposes of war. And if the said Robert with the army of London shall continue for the space of a year at the siege of any town or castle, he shall have 100 shillings from the commonalty of London, and no more. These are the rights of the said Robert in times of war; in times of peace they are as follows:—

'That is to say, the said Robert shall have a soke or ward in the said City, viz., from the wall of the canonry of St. Paul, as a man goes by the Bracine (brew-house) of St. Paul to the Thames, and so to the side of the mill standing by the water that runs down by Fleet Bridge, and thence by the wall, round about the Friers preachers to Ludgate, and so return by the back of the said Fryers' House, to the corner of the said canons' walls of St. Paul. That is to say, all the parish of the church of St. Andrew, which is in his gift in right of his lordship. Appendant to his soke he hath all these things underwritten :—

"That he shall have a Soke-man of his own choice, provided he be of the Sokemannery of the Ward, and if any of the Sokemannery be impleaded at the Guildhall, his sokeman may demand a court of the said Robert, which shall be granted by the Mayor and Citizens. And if any thief be taken in his soke, he shall have stocks and prison in the soke and be taken hence to the Guildhall before the Mayor of judgment, but which shall not be pronounced until he is brought into the court of the said Robert and Franchise; and if the judgment be death for treason he shall be tied to a post in the Thames for two tides, and if he be a common Larcin he shall be hanged at the Elms and there suffer his judgment, as other thieves. Also the said Robert and his heirs have a great honour in holding such a franchise in the said City, where the Mayor and Citizens ought to do him right, that is to say, that when the Mayor is minded to call a great council he shall call the said Robert or his heirs thereto, and he shall be sworn thereof against all people saving the king and his heirs. And when the said Robert cometh to the Hustings of the Guildhall of the said City, the Mayor or his Lieutenant shall arise against him and set him down near to him ; and so long as he is in the Guildhall all the judgments shall be pronounced by him, according to the records of the Recorders of the said Guildhall. And all the waifs which shall happen whilst he is there he shall give to the bailiffs of the City or to whomsoever he pleases, by advice of the Mayor of said City."

Robert, second baron, died in 1328, three years after his father.

Sir John, Kt., third baron, died in 1361, who was knighted for his bravery in war.

Walter, fourth baron, died in 1386. In the 44th Edward III., he was captured when fighting in Gascony, and was obliged to mortgage one of his castles for £1,000 to raise money for his ransom. He held many other military employments.

Walter, fifth baron, died in 1407, having married Joane, sister and heiress of John, second Baron Devereux, who died in 1379, when the Baronies of Fitzwalter and Devereux became united, Walter Fitzwalter becoming Baron Devereux, *jure uxoris*, his heir succeeding in his own right.

Humphrey, sixth baron, died *s.p.*, a minor, in 1422. Walter, his brother, seventh baron, was summoned from 1429 and died in 1432, the last of the line of the Fitzwalters. He fought under Henry V. in the French wars with great distinction, and for his services had a grant of lands in Normandy. His daughter and heiress, Elizabeth, conveyed the baronies by marriage to Sir John Radcliffe, Kt., an eminent military commander, who became Baron Fitzwalter, *jure uxoris*. Dying 39th Henry VI., he was succeeded by his son, Sir John, Kt., who was beheaded in 1495 for implication in the Perkin Warbeck Conspiracy, attainted, and the barony forfeited. Nevertheless, his son, Robert, finding favour at the court of Henry VII. was restored in blood and estates; and in the 1st Henry VIII. to the forfeited barony. For bravery in the French Wars, and other services to the State, he was created Viscount Fitzwalter in 1529, and four years after further elevated in the peerage to the Earldom of Sussex, and was decorated with the order of the Garter. He was thrice married, having issue by all his wives, and died in 1542, when he was succeeded by his eldest son, Sir Henry, K.B. and K.G., who died in 1556, from whom descended Sir Edward, sixth Viscount and Earl, who died, *s.p.*, 1641, when these honours became extinct, the barony falling into abeyance, as it remained during the civil wars and after the Restoration, until 1669, when it was called out, in the person of Benjamin Mildmay, descended from Frances, second daughter of Sir Henry, second Earl of Sussex, who married Sir Thomas Mildmay, of Mulsho, Essex. He died in 1679, was succeeded by his eldest son Charles, who died *s.p.* 1728, to whom followed his brother Henry, who in 1730 was created Viscount Harwich and Earl Fitzwalter; but dying, in 1753, without surviving issue, the two latter titles became extinct, and the barony fell into abeyance, which was terminated in 1868, in the person of Sir Brook William Bridges, fifth baronet, who was called to the House of Peers as Baron Fitzwalter, of Woodham Walter, in the county of Essex, and who died in December, 1875. Having thus disposed of the Barons, Viscounts, and Earls Fitzwalter, it becomes us to inquire into the subsequent history of the old Norman castle, which, flinging its shadow over the then silvery Thames, was the home of the Castellans of London. We have no record of what the Castle of Ralph Baynard was like, but may presume that it was in the usual Norman style, heavy and ungainly, and in its general features not unlike that given in Aggas's Map, *temp.* Elizabeth, as it appeared after its restoration in the 15th century. A view of it was published in 1780, and its site is indicated in the map of Baynard Castle Ward in Northouk's *History of London*. It appears to have been a huge, quadrangular block, the body presenting five gabled divisions, with sextangular corner towers, each division and the towers containing two lofty stories, with narrow slits for windows, and rooms in each gable. Little is known of the castle after its alienation to the Dominicans in

1275, until the reign of Henry VI. It appears to have come to the Crown, and was in the possession of Humphrey, Duke of Gloucester, fourth son of King Henry IV., to whom it had probably been granted by that king. In 1428 it was partially destroyed by fire, but was re-edified by the duke, who continued to reside within its walls until his death. Incurring the jealousy and hatred of Margaret of Anjou and her faction, the duke, who was arrested on a charge of high treason when attending the Parliament of St. Edmundsbury, 1446, at the instance of the queen was committed to prison, and there murdered by suffocation or strangulation, when the castle reverted to the Crown.

In 1460 the Earl of Warwick defeated the Lancastrians at the second battle of St. Alban's, the result of which was a deputation to Edward. Earl of March, now Duke of York, and living in Baynard Castle, to request him to assume the Crown; and it was from its portals that he went in procession to St. Paul's to hear the *Te Deum* sung for the Yorkist Victory, and hence to Westminster, to be vested in the mantle of Royalty, after which he summoned a great council of barons and ecclesiastics to Baynard

Castle, to consult with them on the state of the realm. Richard, Duke of Gloucester, was residing in Baynard Castle, after the murder of his nephews, when he was waited upon by the Lord Mayor and Aldermen of London, for the purpose of requesting him to assume the Crown. Shakespeare delineates the scene with wonderfully graphic power in his drama of *King Richard III.*, act 3, scene 7.

King Henry VII. occupied the castle as a place of residence some three or four years; and Henry VIII. expended large sums of money in repairs and embellishment, and entertained there the King of Castile, but appears to have granted it to the Earl of Pembroke, a gentleman of the bedchamber, who had married Anne, sister of Queen Katherine Parr. On the death of Edward VI. he favoured the pretensions of Lady Jane Grey to the Crown, but almost immediately changed his opinion; and in his City castle a council was held, where it was determined that Mary, King Edward's sister, should succeed, and she was at once proclaimed Queen at Cheapside Cross. In the reign of Elizabeth it appears to have been occupied by Sir John Fortescue, master of the wardrobe, close by, and the Queen is said to have supped there occasionally. It afterwards became the town residence of the Earls of Shrewsbury, coming to that family, probably, through the marriage of John, the tenth earl, with Mary, daughter of Sir Francis Fortescue, and so remained until the Great Fire of 1666, when the venerable old castle, which had witnessed so many important and tragical events connected with the City of which it was the guardian, was finally, and for ever, destroyed, not a vestige now remaining.

Sir Nicholas Brember, Knight, Lord Mayor of London.

EDWARD III. was one of the greatest of English kings, and the progenitor, by Philippa of Hainault, of a family of stalwart sons, brave warriors and able statesmen, whose names will long live in the annals of England and the poetry of romance. They were Edward the Black Prince, the hero of Creci and Poictiers; Lionel, Duke of Clarence; John of Gaunt, "time-honoured Lancaster," titular king of Castile, father of King Henry IV. and of two queens, and the most conspicuous figure in the pages of Froissart; and Thomas, Duke of Gloucester, the most persistent opponent of his nephew, King Richard, and his government by favourites.

Unfortunate was it for England that the Prince of Wales died prematurely, and equally unfortunate was it that he left behind him a son, by the quondam "fair maid of Kent," who succeeded to the throne of his grandfather as Richard II. at eleven years of age, A.D. 1377. In his nonage a council was appointed for the government of the realm, from which all his uncles, the best fitted by affinity and great abilities for the office, were excluded; a measure which gave rise to jealousy and antagonism on their part to his government, with disastrous results to the king's favourites, and ultimately to the king himself. Richard was spoilt by adulation and flattery, and became the tool of intriguers; never displaying much ability, caring more for the display of his grandeur than for the good government of his people; desiring to rule absolutely, but lacking the power; impetuous, fierce, revengeful, and weak-minded, and attempting to accomplish by crooked ways what would have been better carried out by straightforward measures. His chief favourites were Robert de Vere, ninth Earl of Oxford, created Marquis of Dublin in 1386, and Duke of Ireland the following year; Michael de la Pole, a Hull merchant, created Baron de la Pole 1366 and Earl of Suffolk 1385; Alexander Nevill (a younger son of Ralph, second Baron Nevill), Archbishop of York; Sir Robert Tresilian, Chief Justice; and Sir Nicholas Brember, Knight, alderman of London.

Sir Nicholas was a merchant of London of considerable wealth and influence. He is styled by Froissart, "King's Draper," but seems rather to have been a wholesale merchant. Towards the end of the reign of Edward III. the ancient trade-guilds, crafts and mysteries which had hitherto been confined, each to one special trade, were reconstructed as Livery Companies, by charter, and endowed with certain privileges and immunities; as the means of developing commerce.

From *Rot Parl.* ii. 278, it appears that at this period, certain wholesale merchants established the "Grossers' Company," which threatened to ruin some of the smaller crafts. In a petition, 36 Edward III., it is stated that "great mischief had arisen, as well to the king, as to the great men and commons, from the merchants called Grossers, who engrossed all manner of merchandize vendible, and who suddenly raised the price of such merchandize within the realm, putting to sale, by covin and by ordinances, made by themselves, and keeping goods in store till times of dearth, etc.," suggesting as a remedy that these merchants should not be permitted to deal in more than one class of these commodities; and an Act based upon this suggestion was passed 37 Edward III. Although Brember was one of the original members of this monopolizing company, he enforced the penalties provided by the Act with great strictness, as, when he was Lord Mayor in 1385, he disfranchised several freemen for carrying on trades other than their own.

At this time the aldermen were elected annually until 17 Richard II., when they were chosen for life, or during good behaviour. Brember, who had been elected several years in succession, served the office of sheriff in 1372, and that of Lord Mayor not less than four times —in the years 1377, 1383, 1384, and 1385, being the first alderman who held the office in two consecutive years. This, however, was not by the goodwill of the freemen, but in opposition of their wishes, the citizens being favourers of the Duke of Gloucester, and disliking Brember as one of the evil counsellors of the king. In the *Chronicle of London*, printed 1827, from a MS. in the British Museum, is the following passage: —"Also this yere Sr. Nicholl Brembre was chosen Maire agene be the saide craftes, and by men of the contre at Harrow and the contre there aboughte, and not be fre eleccion of the citee of London, as it owith to be; and the olde halle was stuffed with men at armes overe even be ordinaunce and assente of Sr Nicholl Brember fur to chose hym maire on the morrowe, and so he was." This interference with the rights of free election was not allowed to pass without remonstrance. "The folke of the Mercerye" made it the subject of a petition to the King, in which they stated that "Though the eleccion of mairelte was to be to the fremen of the citee bi gode and paisable avys of the wysest and trewest, at a day in the yere, frelich," (free) "Nichol Brembre wyth his upberers, had through debate and stronger partye and carrying grete quantities of armure to the Guyldehall," overawed the citizens and procured his re-election, adding that they of the Mercery or other crafts protested against the election as illegal, "they were anon apeched for arrysers ageins the pees" (impeached as the disturbers of the peace). Although Brember's election was not set aside, this and other remonstrances led to certain reforms in the Corporation.

In 1381 the memorable meeting between King Richard and the Kentish rebels took place in Smithfield, when their leader, Wat Tyler, was stabbed by Lord Mayor Walworth, and when the boy king, by a bold and masterly act, appeased the mob, who were preparing to avenge the death of their captain. Speed informs us that Walworth, after the fall of Tyler, rushed into the City and returned accompanied by Sir Robert Knowles and a thousand citizens in armour, when he "commanded the head of Wat Tyler to be chopt of from his dead carcase and borne before him on a speare to the king." Froissart says, "among the first" (from the City) "came Sir Robert Knolles and Sir Perducas d'Albret well attended, then several aldermen, with upwards of 600 men at arms, and a powerful man of the City, by name Nicholas Brember, the king's draper, bringing with him a large force on foot." After the dispersion of the mob with ample promises of a redress of their grievances, the king knighted Walworth, and gave him a fee farm worth £100 per annum, as he did also Aldermen Brember, Philpot, Laund, Standish, Twiford, and Traver, granting to each a fee farm of £40 per annum. Thomas of Woodstock, the king's youngest uncle, created Duke of Gloucester, 1385, was the most vehement opponent of his nephew's policy, and the favourites Vere, Pole, and Brember, perceiving him to be the greatest obstacle to their assumption of the supreme direction of affairs conspired to remove him. They arranged that he should be invited to a supper in Brember's house, and whilst there should be assassinated. It was, however, necessary that the invitation should be sent through Lord Mayor Exton, "who," says Maitland, "was no sooner acquainted with this wicked design than he received it with the utmost abhorrence and detestation, and boldly declared that he would never consent to so flagitious an act of villainy," and forthwith gave information to the duke, who took measures for his safety, and resolved upon the destruction of the conspirators, in which he was backed by the citizens of London, who suggested that he should assume the government of the country, hinting that they would be ready to give him support. This, however, was not a practicable scheme, for even if York and Lancaster should approve of the deposition of Richard, they, as elder brothers, would have prior claims to the succession.

The question was brought before the Parliament of 1386, which met at Westminster, when a council of eleven, with Gloucester at the head, was appointed to govern the kingdom under the king, who was required to dismiss Pole, his chancellor, and the rest of his favourites, which he promised to do, but as soon as Parliament broke up he carried them with him into the west of England to devise measures for opposing the confederacy. They resolved to take up arms against the duke, and, as a preliminary, called a council of the judges at Nottingham, who, under compulsion, declared the acts of the Parliament invalid, and those who passed them traitors. Whilst at Bristol the king sent Pole, Brember, and Sir Peter Gouloufre to London for intelligence, where they had an interview with the governor of the Tower, who told them that they ran great risk in coming there. "How so," they inquired; "we are the king's knights, and have a right of entry into his palaces?" The governor replied "that it was true the Tower belonged to the king, and that he would be obedient to him, but could no further than when his orders were not in contravention to the will of the council and the Duke of Gloucester; and (added he) I tell you for your welfare that you had better depart, for if it become known that you are here, the Tower will be besieged by the citizens, and you will be torn to pieces." Upon hearing this they departed, not caring to brave the fury of a London mob, returned to Kensington, mounted their horses, and rode back to the king.

Meanwhile Gloucester and his nephew, the Earl of Derby, afterwards King Henry IV., finding that none but the most decided measures would prevail with the king, raised an army of 40,000 men, with which they marched towards London—not with the object of dethroning the king, but to uphold the council and destroy the power of the favourites. Richard, who was not deficient in boldness, came to London, and it was reported that Brember and Sir Thomas Trivet accompanied him with a thousand armed men, who were secretly placed in the mews at Charing Cross, with the view of killing the most obnoxious of the king's enemies as they passed from London to Westminster.

Richard kept state in Westminster Hall, and when he was informed of the rumours relative to Brember and his thousand men, swore solemnly that he knew nothing about them, but contrived to get them away and join De Vere in the West, who was raising an army in Wales in the king's service.

When the lords presented themselves before the king, the Bishop of Ely, the new Lord Chancellor, asked them why they were assembled in warlike array at Haringey Park, to whom they replied, "For the good of the king and the kingdom, and to weed out the traitors by whom he is surrounded." On being asked to name the traitors, they answered, "Robert de Vere, Duke of Ireland; Alex. Nevill, Archbishop of York; Michael de la Pole, Earl of Suffolk; Sir Robert Tresilian, that false Justicier; and Sir Nicholas Brember, that false knight of London;" and then threw down the gage of challenge. The king, having sent his favourites out of immediate harm's way, rated the lords soundly for presuming to take up arms against his supreme will and authority. "You," said he, "whom I could kill like cattle, and whom I esteem no more than the basest scullion in my kitchen!" yet he eventually promised that the matter should be taken into consideration by the Parliament, which would assemble at Westminster on the morrow after Candlemas.

A proclamation was soon after issued by Richard, forbidding any one, under pain of death, to supply arms, ammunition, or provisions to the rebel army, and he sent word to De Vere to hasten his muster of men, and march towards London to put down the rebellion. Simultaneously with the proclamation, the confederates sent a letter to the Corporation of London, soliciting their sympathy and aid, which was immediately responded to with assurances of both.

The Duke of Ireland, with his Welsh army, marched eastward and came to Oxford, when he heard that the Dukes of Gloucester and York and Lord Mayor Exton were coming to meet him, and were not far distant, having crossed the Thames by Reading Bridge—those of Staines and Windsor having been broken down by direction of de Vere. He had been appointed Lieut.-General of the king's forces, with Suffolk and Brember in command under him; but on hearing this intelligence he became terribly alarmed. He called a council of war, and it was decided that they must give battle to the enemy; but it was also arranged that they—De Vere, De la Pole, and Brember—should station themselves on fleet horses in the wings of the army, so that if the day went against them, they might save themselves by flight.

Soon afterwards the army of Gloucester made

its appearance, and the King's Welshmen, panic stricken, threw down their arms, and took to flight in disorder. Their leaders followed—or set the example—and escaped to Wales, and hence De Vere, De la Pole, and the Archbishop gained the Continent by way of Scotland, the Duke of Ireland dying an exile in Holland, Suffolk in France, and Nevill as a parish priest in Flanders. With respect to the others. Froissart says: "Brember was arrested in Wales, brought to London, and beheaded:" Speed: "Sir N. Brember and others were aprehended, and kept in straight prison to answere such accusations (which if meere calumniations) as in the next Parliament at Westminster, should be objected. Parliament met at Candlemas; Tresilian had sentence to be drawn to Tyburne in the afternoone, and there to have his throat cut, which was done accordingly. This Bramber" (saith Walsingham) " was saide to have imagined to bee made Duke of New Troye (the olde supposed name of London), by murthering thousands of such citizens (whose names he had billed for that purpose) as were of such likelihood to oppose him." Maitland says, "Soon after Nicholas Brember, late Lord Mayor of London, one of the wicked favourites of Richard, was condemned by Parliament for High Treason, for which he was adjudged to be drawn and hanged, which was accordingly executed upon him at Tyburn, and not according to that idle story mentioned by Holingshed, Stow, and others, of his being beheaded with an ax, which he had prepared for the execution of all such as opposed his measures. If this perfidious and cruel man and his accomplices had succeeded in their wicked schemes he was to have been made Duke of New Troye, as London is denominated by the fabulous Geoffrey of Monmouth."

Brember was buried in Christ Church, Newgate Street. His arms are emblazoned in the Hall of the Grocers' Company.

An Olden Time Bishop of London: Robert de Braybrooke.

IN the pleasant Northamptonshire village of Braybrooke, on the verge of a forest, and near the Leicestershire border, there was born, some five-and-a-half centuries ago, a child who was destined to pass his name down to posterity in the annals of London.

In the earlier portion of the thirteenth century, Robert May, otherwise de Braybrooke, a favourite of King John, and landed proprietor in Braybrooke, built a castle on his estates for his residence. His eldest son, Henry, married Christian Ledlet, a great heiress, and assumed the name of Ledlet. The estates passed by marriage to the Griffin family, who were created Barons de Braybrooke, 1688, the barony expiring for lack of male heirs, 1742; but the heiress married William Whitwell, whose son assumed the name of Griffin and was created Baron Braybrooke, 1788, with limitation to his nephew, Richard Neville Aldworth, who succeeded to the barony, and assumed the name of Neville in addition to and after Aldworth, from whom is descended the extant Baron Braybrooke. Henry de Braybrooke, probably the son of Robert, was a "justice itinerant" in county Beds, and was dragged from the bench at Dunstable by the Norman Falcasius—who held Bedford Castle for the King against the barons—and cast into a dungeon of the castle for having given adverse judgments in thirty-five law suits which had been instituted by Falcasius.

The boy Robert was probably born in the castle, and educated in the little monastery in the forest hard by, or possibly in the more distant great abbey of Medehamsted (Peterborough), and in his youthful wanderings would doubtless sometimes visit the neighbouring town of Lutterworth, where Wyclif, the leader of the Lollards, Braybrooke's victims, was afterwards to pass away from this world.

After his preliminary studies he went to Oxford, where he became a licentiate of civil law, and took Holy Orders.

His very first act after ordination displays his character as a determined supporter of Papal supremacy, and at the same time demonstrates the influence of his family. In spite of the statute of provisors, recently passed, and of præmunire, he obtained a provision from the Pope for induction into the living of Hinton, in Cambridgeshire, the patronage being vested in the Fellows of Peterhouse; and notwithstanding the penalties attaching to the offence, obtained the living in 1360, and held it nineteen years. In 1366, he was nominated Prebendary of Fenton, in York Cathedral, which he exchanged for that of Friday Thorpe in the same cathedral, 1376, and the same year was appointed Archdeacon of Cornwall, and Prebendary of Wells. In 1380, he was constituted Dean of Salisbury, and a few months after exchanged his archdeaconry for the rectory of Bideford, resigning at the same time the rectory of Hinton. The following year, by virtue of a Bull of Pope Urban VI., he was appointed sixty-third Bishop of London, succeeding Courtney, who had been translated to Canterbury in place of Archbishop Sudbury, who had been beheaded on Tower Hill three months before by the Wat Tyler insurgents.

Braybrooke lived in one of the most important periods in the annals of England—a transition period—when the religious, political, and intellectual systems of the country were experiencing earthquake-throes, essential in working out that liberty and social civilization which we now enjoy.

In the early portion of his life, the throne was occupied by "the greatest of the Plantagenets;" in his middle life, by one of the weakest; and the latter portion witnessed that change of dynasty which resulted in the Wars of the Roses, sweeping off vast numbers of the Norman lords, and leaving England more Saxon than it had been since the Conquest. In the century preceding his birth the feudal barons had been struggling with John and Henry III. against oppressive monarchial prerogative; had wrested from John the Magna Charta; and under the leading of Simon de Montfort, had in the latter reign summoned the first representative Parliament. And now the mass of the people—who had remained serfs, mere chattels, who could be bought and sold like cattle—rose under Wat Tyler and Jack Straw to assert their rights, proclaiming that all men were by nature equally free, and demanding the abolition of serfdom, the abrogation of unjust and oppressive laws, open markets, etc., adopting as their motto,—

> "When Adam delved, and Eve span,
> Who was then the gentleman?"

Their demands eventuated in certain concessions; but it was not until the Stuarts, by their exaggerated notions of kingly prerogative, had precipitated rebellion, that the liberties of England were established on a sure foundation by the victories of Cromwell. It was the period, too, of the commencement of the struggle with Rome for liberty of conscience. Never had England sunk so low in degradation as in 1213, when John, after boldly defying the Pope, found himself compelled to lay his crown at the feet of Pandulph. But now, "the morning star of the Reformation" was, by voice and pen, awakening the people to a consciousness of their slavery to a foreign priest, proclaiming that the Scriptures were the only rule of faith, and asserting the right of private judgment. Under the vigorous rule of the third Edward, the authority of the Pope in the realm was materially curbed, and enactments made declaring John's submission illegal, lacking, as it did, the assent of the representatives of the people, and making it penal to publish bulls, or any other Papal instruments, in the kingdom without the consent of Parliament.

Nevertheless the Lollards were looked upon as heretics by the authorities of the Church, and in 1377, Wyclif was cited to appear before the Primate and Bishop Courtnay in St. Paul's Cathedral. He went thither accompanied by his patrons, John of Gaunt and the Earl Marshal (Lord Henry Percy), when the latter, in consideration of the age and feebleness of the venerable reformer, desired him to be seated, "which," says Foxe, "eftsoons cast the Bishop of London into a furious chafe," which resulted in an altercation, the abrupt breaking up of the assembly, and the rush of the London mob, with whom the Duke of Lancaster was not then popular, to his palace of the Savoy, where they murdered a priest, but were dispersed by the Lord Mayor.

After the murder of Archbishop Sudbury and the elevation of Courtnay to the primacy, he called a synod together at the House of the Preaching Friars, London, at which the new bishop (Braybrooke) attended. Soon after their assembling, a shock of an earthquake occurred, which alarmed the ecclesiastics, but Courtnay adroitly turned it to account, saying that earthquakes were but the expulsion of noxious vapours from the earth, and it was a sign that Heaven looked with approval on their efforts to expel noxious doctrines from the Church, and the meeting very speedily pronounced fourteen of Wyclif's tenets erroneous or heretical.

This was, however, but the seed-time of religious liberty; the seeds, nevertheless, in spite of opposition, fructified under Henry VIII. and his daughter Elizabeth, grew apace under the Commonwealth, and the harvest was reaped after the expulsion of the second James.

Intellectually, too, Braybrooke was the contemporary of the transition from ignorance to learning. Chaucer, in his *Canterbury Pilgrims*, and Gower in his *Confessio Amantis*, were laying the foundation of our modern language and literature; and Faust, Gutenberg, and Schœffer were establishing their printing presses in Germany, to be introduced into England by Caxton in the next century, to aid in the diffusion of knowledge, and in the liberation of the people from political and spiritual thraldom.

When Braybrooke, half a millennium ago, was elevated to the episcopal bench, London was a comparatively small city, encircled by two miles of walls, gates, and ditch, with but one bridge over the Thames—that built by Peter of Colechurch, with its movable centre for the passage of vessels. The Tower was the Court and king's residence; with Baynard's Castle, in Thames Street; the magnificent Palace of the Savoy, the Monastery of the Knights Hospitallers, in Clerkenwell, and many another noble edifice lay in ruins, demolished by the Wat Tyler insurgents; the city was crowded with monasteries and churches; and the streets presented a mingled crowd of nobles, monks, friars, priests, and merchant burghers.

His cathedral was that which had risen on the ruins of the one destroyed by fire in the reign of the Conqueror, which had been 200 years in course of erection, and now stood forth a grand building, covering four acres of ground, with its Norman nave, two transepts, its pointed Gothic choir, its spire, 510 feet in height, and its beautiful Ladye Chapel, majestic in its magnitude, and beautiful in some of its details; with St. Paul's cross outside, where, every Sunday, some eloquent friar or priest addressed the citizens; and where many a memorable political sermon has been preached. On the northern side, near

Warwick Lane, stood his residence, the Bishop's palace, described as being "a stately and spacious pile."

Internally he found the ecclesiastics in a lax state of discipline, and "the house of God a den of thieves." The cathedral was devoted more to secular than to religious uses. "The south alley for usury, the north for simony, and a horse fair in the midst, for all kinds of bargains, meetings, brawlings, murthers, and conspiracies; and the font for the payment of money;" which were associated with the shooting of arrows, ball playing, and deeds even more reprehensible than these. These abuses he set himself to correct, and effected a great reformation. The sacred edifice was also a sort of theatre, where mystery and miracle plays were performed, the stage consisting of three platforms, the upper representing the Creator, surrounded by angels; the second occupied by apostles, saints, and martyrs; and the lower presenting the mouth of hell, vomiting flames and smoke, and resounding with the shrieks of the lost. But it pleased the taste of the age that the monarch of the nether regions should correspond with the clown of the modern pantomime; and in the midst of solemn passages,

s

the devil, with a troupe of his imps, would issue forth, to perform all sorts of antics, and regale the ears of the audience with drolleries, filth, and what would now be considered blasphemy. With these representations the bishop did not interfere, considering them the only mode of appealing to the hearts and consciences of the ignorant multitude; unless, indeed, he sanctioned the petition of St. Paul's Players to Richard II., to prohibit ignorant and inexperienced persons from "acting the History of the Old Testament to the prejudice of the clergy of the Church." A favourite device of these plays was the descent of a white dove from an aperture of the roof, with the swinging of censers, to represent the descent of the Third Person in the Trinity.

On the surrender of the chancellorship by Sir Richard Scrope, 1382, "Robert Braybrooke, Bishopp of London," says Speed, "was made chancellor in his place. This act of the King's was displeasant to the whole realme, and one of the first things by which hee fell into dislike, it being among the infelicities of King Richard that those times were too full of sower and impatient censors for a Prince of so calme a temper, and as yet unseasoned in yeares, but hee onely held the office a yeare."

The distinguishing characteristic of Braybrooke's career was his unrelenting persecution of the Lollards. It was enacted, 5 Richard II., that any person preaching against the Catholic Faith should be imprisoned until he could "justify himself;" and 2 Henry IV. that all persons "suspected" of heresy should be imprisoned until they were "canonically purged," or until they abjured their errors, and that if they persisted in their heresy they should be delivered to the secular arm and "burnt to death before the people." Toleration was a word not known in that age. The oppressed ever cried out for liberty of conscience, whether Romanist or Reformer, but when they became the dominant power they were alike intolerant: and the cruelties of the bishop to the Lollards must be ascribed to the spirit of the age, backed by his own intense conviction that the Romanist was the one "sole Apostolic Church," and that to destroy the enemies who were beleaguering her was doing a service to God.

The bishop appears to have always been on friendly terms with the citizens of London, and was, with the Duke of Gloucester, instrumental in the reconciliation of King Richard and the Corporation after their serious quarrel about a loan of £1,000, afterwards heading a procession of 400 citizens on horseback to tender their submission, on which occasion a fountain of wine was set playing at the door of the cathedral, and the streets presented an animated spectacle, with streaming banners and tapestries hanging in front of the houses, the whole enlivened with instrumental music.

Notwithstanding his conservative sentiments, he welcomed the landing of Bolingbrooke, assisted actively in the deposition of Richard, was one of the signers of the document consigning him to perpetual imprisonment, which meant death, within the walls of " bloody Pomfret," and crowned the usurper ; afterwards conducting a service in St. Paul's, at which King Henry was present, when the corpse of the murdered Richard was exposed there, to certify to the citizens that he was really dead, and obviate the possibility of revolts in his name.

Bishop Braybrooke died in the year 1404 (his epitaph says 1405), and he was buried in the Ladye Chapel of his cathedral, under "a faire marble stone inlaide with letters made every one of a several piece of brasse." Two-and-a-half centuries after his burial the cathedral was destroyed in the great fire of London, and on the removal of the rubbish for the rebuilding the tomb was found open, with the slab broken. "The body," as Camden states, "was found entire, the skin still inclosing the bones and fleshy parts; only in the breast there was a hole (made, I suppose, by accident) through which one might view and handle his lungs. The skin was of deep tawny colour and the body very light, as appeared to all who came to view and touch it, it being exposed in a coffin for some time without any offensive smell: and then reinterred."

A Brave Old London Bishop: Fulco Basset.

AT the period when this prelate lived, England was struggling to free itself from the shackles of its Norman and Angevin rulers. The feudal system had been introduced at the Conquest, which constituted the king the absolute master of the land; the barons were his vassals, holding their lands by tenures of military service, and the great mass of the people were either vassals of the barons, holding portions of land by knight's service, or were mere serfs, excepting some merchants and traders in the cities and towns, who enjoyed a modified species of freedom, for which special charters were granted by kings. The citizens of London have ever been famous for the bold and resolute way in which they have preserved and defended the liberties and immunities granted in such charters, and when Basset became their bishop they gladly welcomed him as one who would not be backward in lending them his countenance and assistance in any attempted invasion of their chartered rights.

Beyond this permissive freedom, however, they aimed at something further; the notion that kings were not the masters, but the servants, of the sovereign people had been bruited abroad, and the initiative had been taken by the barons, who revolted against the tyranny of John, and extorted from him the Magna Charta, in which they were backed by the Londoners and the merchants of other large towns; but the peasantry and labourers were too much down-trodden in serfdom to make any assertion of their natural rights, and it was not until more than a century afterwards that they, under Wat Tyler, Jack Cade, and other leaders, began to put forth the strange notion that they also were men with natural rights, which they ceased not to reiterate, until a couple of centuries afterwards they established their claims at Marston Moor and Naseby and Worcester.

Thurstan Basset came to England at the Conquest, whose descendant Ralph (*temp*. Henry II.,) by his great abilities raised the family to distinction and wealth, and was the author of many salutary laws, notably that of Frank Pledge. From him issued three baronies by writ, those of Basset of Sapcoate, 1264-1378; Basset of Drayton, 1264, in abeyance 1390; and Basset of Welden, 1299-1410.

Thomas, his second son, was founder of the Wycombe branch, whose eldest son, Gilbert, had issue by Egeline, daughter of — Courtney, three sons—Gilbert, Fulco, and Philip—all of whom succeeded to the paternal estates, one after the other.

Fulco was born at the end of the 12th century, was brought up to the Church, and became Provost of Beverley, 1206-1238; Rector of Cottesbrook, Northants, which he resigned, 1239; Dean of York, 1239-1242; Bishop of London, 1241-1258, but not consecrated until 1244, in consequence of a vacancy in the See of Canterbury. He died of the plague, 1258, and was buried in St. Paul's Cathedral.

In the year 1250, he had a warm altercation with the Archbishop of Canterbury, relative to metropolitical visitation, to which the archbishop had an undoubted right, but which Basset denied. "Comming to London, Boniface (the archbishop) tooke a small occasion to defoce the bishop with fowle and reprochfull speeches, and being resisted by the Dean and Chapter of Paules (who had appealed from his visitation to the Pope), he made no more adoo but excommunicated them every one." The next day he proceeded to the priory of St. Bartholomew, in Smithfield, telling the sub-prior and monks, who came in their copes to meet him, that he had come to visit them, who replied very respectfully that "they knew their bishop (whose only office it was) to be a very sufficient man in his place," and that, "although they were sorry to disappoint him, they could not recognise any other." "This answere so enraged this lusty Archbishop, as not being able to containe his anger within any bounds of discretion, he ranne violently to the Sub Prior, strucke the poore old man downe to the ground, kicked him, beate him and buffeted him pitifully, tore his coape from his backe, rent it into a number of pieces, and when he had so done stamped upon it like a madde man." His followers also fell upon the monks, and a general fight took place; but the Londoners hearing of the fray took up cudgels in behalf of their bishop and prior, when the archbishop took to flight, and got safely across the ferry to Lambeth. "If they (the Londoners) could have met with him, they would surely have hewen him into a thousand peeces." As soon as he got home he excommunicated the whole of the inmates of the priory, and along with them Bishop Basset. Appeals on both sides were made to Rome, the Dean of St Paul's going thither, followed by the archbishop. A great deal of bribery took place, the Pope pocketing the proceeds from both parties alike, and delaying his decision in order to exact more money, which seems not to have been spared. At length he gave judgment that the archbishop had the right of visitation all through his province, but for the unseemly brawling and fighting in Smithfield he condemned him to rebuild, at his own cost, Lambeth Palace, which was then in a dilapidated condition.

Although he was ever zealous and earnest in his defence of the people against kingly and priestly tyranny, and supported the barons in this and the preceding reign, it was in his old age, when verging upon the grave, that Basset especially made a display of that bravery and sturdy English love of freedom and hatred of oppression which entitles him to the designation at the head of this chapter.

King Henry and the Pope had conspired together to levy a tax on the English clergy, and share the plunder. Rustand, the Pope's legate, with this view, convoked a meeting of the clergy of London, and made his demand in the name of the Pope. Basset rose and replied, in unmeasured terms, on the illegality and oppressive nature of the exaction, finishing by saying that rather than submit to so intolerable a demand he would lose his head, and in this he was backed by his clergy, who passed an unanimous resolution to ignore any such claim altogether. The legate laid his complaint before the king, who sent for the bishop, abused him with vile and menacing language, and threatened him with deprivation and Papal censure. Basset listened meekly to all the king had to say, but when he left his presence he said to those who he knew would carry it to the king, "He may remove my mitre, if it so pleases him, but he will find a helmet beneath it, and he may take away my crosier, but that is easily replaced with a sword."

M. Paris says of him, "He was a noble and honourable man, and, excepting his last slip, the anchor of the whole kingdom, and the shield of stability and defence." Weever also says, "As he was a man of great lineage, and also of ample —both temporal and ecclesiastical—possessions, so was he a prelate of an invincible, high spirit; stout and courageous to resist those insupportable exactions which the Pope's legate, Rustandus, went about to lay upon the clergie."

In the year 1256 he commenced the erection of the church of St. Faith, under St. Paul's cathedral, founded a charity in St. Paul's for the repose of his soul, and bequeathed to the cathedral a golden apple, two carved chests for relics, some vestments, and a few manuscripts.

An Old London Diarist.

IN the sixteenth century there dwelt in the parish of Holy Trinity the Less, Queenhithe, a worthy and honest citizen, one Henry Machyn, a member of the Merchant Taylors' Company. He was born about the period of the accession of Henry VIII., and lived until after the accession of Elizabeth, dying, it is presumed, in 1563, of the plague which visited London in that year, when his diary comes to an abrupt conclusion.

The age in which he lived was a most important period, that of the transition from Popery to Protestantism, accompanied by the discords, troubles, evil passions, and cruelties incidental to transitional epochs. During his life, he witnessed not less than three changes in the national faith: First, the rejection of the Papal supremacy, the suppression of monasteries, and the establishment of the reformed religion under Henry VIII.; secondly, a return to the old Papal allegiance and faith at the accession of Mary; and thirdly, the final downfall of Popery, under

Elizabeth. Our diarist, although, like the Vicar of Bray, he seems to have accommodated his conscience to the prevailing religion, evidently had a leaning towards the old faith, which is manifested by the gusto with which he describes the Church ceremonies and regal pageants of Mary's reign, and the "sarve them right" sort of style in which he records the pillorying, whipping at cart-tails, and lopping off the ears of utterers of "haynous wordes aganst the Queen's magesty," as compared with the somewhat despondent tone of the entries after the accession of Elizabeth.

It would appear, although not stated, that he was a purveyor of trappings for pageants and funerals, heraldic painter, and undertaker in general; his place of business was near to the Painterstainers' Hall and the College of Arms; and it is supposed that he kept several workmen employed in emblazoning flags, pennons, escutcheons, etc., for public processions and spectacles.

The diary at the beginning appears to have been nothing more than a trade record, consisting almost entirely of notices of funerals and the pomp thereof, most probably those which he conducted himself. Afterwards he notices other pageants—Lord Mayors' Shows, Royal processions, guild companies' displays, etc., in most of which he would probably have some professional connexion. Subsequently he records notable events outside his profession, such as "preching at Powlle's Crosse;" changes in religion; proceedings of Queen Mary, her marriage, etc.; the punishing of heretics on the gallows and at the stake; standings in the "pelere;" "rydyngs in Chepe;" penance in churches; and sundry other events of a similarly lively character, which were marked features of the time.

The diary is remarkably free from egotism, being written throughout in the third person, even when speaking of himself or family, which is very seldom. The following entries relate to himself and family: 1. 1550, the funeral of his brother—"30th November was bered Crystoffe Machyn, Marchand Tayllor in the parryche of Sant James and broder of Henry Machyn: the Cumpene of Marchand Tayllors behyng at the berehyng and the Compene of the Clarkes syngyng and—Maydwell dyd pryche for hym." 2. The birth of a daughter. September 25th

1557; he writes that his wife was "browth a 'bed with a whenche," that she was attended by his "gossip Master Harper," who was surgeon accoucheur to the Queen; and that two days after was "chrysten'd Katheryn, doythur of Hare (Harry) Machyn;" further that "Mistress Grenway, an Altherman's wife, and Masters Blakwelle and Grenwell" were the sponsors. 3. A notice of his own doing penance, but recorded in the third person and with a Frenchifying of his name. "November 23rd, 1561: the third yere of Quen Elesabeth, dyd preche at Powlle's crosse, Renager, yt was Sant Clement Day; dyd syt alle the sermon tym Henry des Machyn for two (words) the wyche was tolde hym, that Veron, the French—the precher was taken wyth a wenche, by the reporting, by on (one) Wylliam Lawrence, clark of Sant Mare (Mary) Maudlen, in Mylke Streete; the wych the same Hare (Harry) kneelyd down before Master Veron and the byshopp, and yett (they) would nott for (forgive) hym for alle ys fryndes that he hadde worshepefulle." 4. Marriage of his niece. July 7th, 1562, "that Symon Smith browth to the Gyldhalle, Kynlure Machen for to have lyssens (licence) to have her a husband, Edw. Gardener,

Cowper . . dowther of Cristofer Machyn." These are all the references to himself and family, but there is a memorandum on one of the sheets of a business nature, which indicates his having been an emblazoner of arms : " Rember yt my lade (Lady) Masum byll for armes,"—the rest illegible.

The diary extends from 1550 to 1563; it is couched in language and orthography which denote deficient education even for that time, but is valuable as a reliable record of events, interesting as a picture of the age, and amusing from its quaint style. Strype made great use of it in the way of quotation in his *Ecclesiastical Memorials*, as a trustworthy authority. The MS. is in the Cotton collection. It suffered in the fire at Sir Robert Cotton's house, Westminster, and now remains in a fragmentary form, being much scorched and burnt at the edges. In the year 1848, it was published by the Camden Society, edited by Mr. John Gough Nichols, F.S.A., with a glossary, notes, etc.

The following extracts from the diary give a vivid picture of London 300 years ago; the tone of public opinion, and the turbulence of the time, with the picturesque accessories of pageants and

T

processions, and the less pleasing but ever present spectacles of whipping, pillorying, hanging, quartering, and burning of heretics and rebels.

1. The restored Papal rule. Queen Mary ascended the throne in 1553, and immediately reversed all the doings of her father and brother in matters of religion. Thus writes Machyn:—

"August 5th, 1553. Cam out of the Marselsay the old Bishop of London, Bonar, & dyvers bysshopes bryngyng him unto home ye plasse at Powlces, & doctor Coke whent to the same plass yn the Marselsey that the bysshope was in."

February 12th, 1573-4. After Wyatt's rebellion "there was mad at evere gate in Lundun a newe payre of galous, & set up 11 payre in Cheapside; 11 payre in Fletstrett, 1 in Smythfyld, 1 in Holborne, 1 at Ledyn-hall, 1 at Sant Magnus, London Bridg, one at Refer Allay Gatt, one at Sant George's, 1 at Borunsay (Bermondsey) strett, 1 on Towr hylle, 1 payre at Charyng Crosse, and 1 payre besyd Hyd Parke corner." The executions took place on the 14th, and "on the iiii daye of junii wasse all the galus in London plokyd done in all plases."

September 23rd, 1554. "Dyd pryche doctur

Rud at Powlle's Crosse, and he recantyd and repentyd that he ever was mared (married) and sayd openly that he cold not mare by God's law."

September 15th, 1556. "A sermon was preached at Powlle's," when was declared, "the Popes jubele and pardon from Rome, and as mony as wyll rescyffe ye pardon so to be schryff (shrived) and fast three days in on weeke and to rescyff the blessed sacrament, the next Sunday affter, clen remyssyon of alle ther synnes tossyens quossyens (? *toties quoties*) of all that ever they dyd."

March 25th, 1556. A grand day at Bow Church. "Our Lady Day, the Annunsyasyon, at Bow Chyrch was hangyd wyth cloth of gold and with rich hares (arras) and cossens (cushions) for the commyng of my Lord Cardenal Pole. Ther dyd the Bysshop of Vossetr (Worcester) syng he (high) masse, mytyred, and ther were dyver bysshopes, as the B. of Ely, London, and Lynkkolne, and the Yerle of Pembroke, and Ser Edw. Hastynges, the Master of the Horse, and dyvers odur nobul" (unfinished).

It seems there were those in London who did not approve of the Queen's proceedings, and even resorted to violent measures, besides Sir Thomas Wyatt and his followers. 1554-5. "The 17th day of Feybuary, at about mydnight, ther wer serten lude feylows cam unto Sant Thomas of Acurs, and over the dore ther was set the ymage of Sant Thomas, and ther they brake ys neke and the tope of ys crosier, the wych was mad of fre stone. With grett sham was yt done." On March 14th, the same year, "Serten velyns dyd breke the neke of the ymage of Sant Thomas of Cantarbere, and on of ys arms broke."

The next day was issued, "A proclamassyon that wo so ever cold bring word to the mare who dyd breke ys neke shuld have C. (100) croones of gold for his labur." He does not state whether the iconoclasts were discovered. There are numberless entries also, such as the following: "July 24th, 1553, was a felow set in the pelere [pillory] for speykyng agaynst the good Quen Mare." September 17th, 1557, "Ther whent out of Newgatt unto Yylyngton beyond the buttes, towards the cherche, in a valey, to be borned, four—three men, on woman, for herese duly—two of them was man and wyfe dwellyng in Sant Dunstan's in the East." November 12th, 1658. "Saturday, ther was a woman sett on the pelere for sayhing that the Quen was ded and her Grace was not ded."

After the death of Queen Mary, we read: "August 24th. (The Lord) Mare and the althermen and the (sheriffs) wher at the wrastleyng at Clarke in Well, and it was the fayre daye of thynges kept in Symthfeld, Sant Bathellmuw, and the same daye my lorde (mayor) cam hom through Chepe and agaynst Yrmonger (lane), and agaynst Sant Thomas of Ocurs two gret (bonfires) of rodes (crosses) and of Mares (images of the Virgin Mary) and Johns and odur emages ther they wher bornyd with gret wondur."

Also, in the same year: "The tyme afor Bathell muwtyd and after was alle the rodes (crosses), and Mares and Johns, and many odur of the cherche gudes both copes, crosses, censers, altar-clothes, rod-clothes, bokes, baner-bokes and baner-stays, waynskott wyth myche odur gayre (gear) about London .. (which were all destroyed); and ther was a felow within the chyrche (St. Botolph, Bishopsgate Street) mad a sermon at the bornyng of the chyrch goodes."

2. Funerals.—In describing these the author is

quite at home, with his penons and skotchons, and torchys and blake clokes, which he catalogues minutely. These occupy about half the diary. Be it also observed that Englishmen then, like Englishmen of the nineteenth century, could not assemble for any purpose or conclude any regal or civic procession without a "gret dener."

"May 20th, 1551, was bered my lade (Lady) Hobullthorne, late (Mayoress) of London, with 2 herolds, 4 penons of armes, and ther was (the) clerkes of London, and ther had powre (poor) men and women many fryse gownes, and there was 4 althermen morners, and 2 of them knyghts, and ther a grett doll (dole) was, and the morrow a grett dener, &c."

"March 22nd, 1552, was bered Master John Heth dwellyng in Fanchyrche-strett, and ther went affor him C (100) chyldern of Grayfreers, boys and gyrlles, 2 and 2 together, and he gayff them them shurts and smokes and gyrdulls and moketors; and after thay hadde wy(ne) and fygs and good alle, and ther wor a grett dener; and ther whor the Cumpane of Painters and the clerkes, and ys cumpony had xxs. to make mere (merry) with alle at the taverne."

"October 9th, 1554, was bered Master George Medley, merser and late Chamberlayn of the Cete of London, with 2 whyt branchys and 12 pore men, with 12 stayffes, torchyes, and 12 gownes, and dyvers men and women in blake gownes; and ye comes afore ys body, and the compene of clarkes and of the mersors; and when alle was don they went hom to drynke; and the morrow after the masse of requiem and ther dyd pryche doctur Smyth, and after hom to dener."

In the same year was buried "Richard Townley in Sant Austyn parryche syd Poweles, with 10 torchys and 4 gret (tapers) and 2 whyt branchys with a herold of armes, with a standerd, a penon of armes, cote, elmet, target, sword, the crest, a hawke, and 6 dosen of scochyons and piests and dyrkes."

"September 10th, 1555, was bered my Lade Lyonys, the Mares (Mayoress) of London, with a goodly herse mad in Sant Benet Sherog perryche, with 2 branchys and 24 gownes of blake for pore men and 3 of emages and 6 dosen penselds and 6 dosen of schochyons, and the althermen folohyng the corrse and after the Compane of Grosers, and the morow, the masse, and master H—— did pryche and after a grett dener."

At the burial of Master Robin, of Mark Lane, in Barking church, the street and church being hung with black cloth, and the Lord Mayor and Alderman. After an account of the heraldic and other paraphernalia, he concludes, "and affter they whent to dener for thys was affor none."

The following describes the funeral of Sir John Gresham, uncle to Sir Thomas Gresham, the builder of the Royal Exchange, who was apprenticed to him. He served the office of Sheriff in 1537, and that of Lord Mayor in 1547.

"Oct. 30th, 1556, was bered Ser John Gressem knyght and merser and merchand of the stapul of callys and merchand venterer, and late mare and altherman of London, with a standerd and a penon of armes—armur of damast and 4 pennons of armes—a elmet, a targett, and a sword, mantylles, and—and a goodly herse of wax and 10 dosen of pensils and 12 dosen of scochyons, and he gayff C blake gownes unto pore men and powre women of fyne blake cloth, 3 dosen of grett stayffe torchys, and a dosen of long torchys and he gayff a C.d. (150) of fyne blake—2 unto the mare and the old mare, and to ser Rowland Hylles, and to ser Andrew Jude, and to boyth the chamberlayns, and to the Master of Blakwell, and to Master the common huntt and ys men, and to the porters that longs the stapul, and to alle ys farmers and ys tenantts, and alle the chyrche hangyd and the strett with blake and armes grett store, and morow three goodly masses song, on of the Senete (Trinity) and a nodur of owre lade (Lady), and the third of requiem and a goodly sermon. Master Harpfield dyd pryche, and after as grett a dener as has bene sene for a fysse day (a day of fasting) for alle that came to dener, for ther laket (lacked) nothyng dere."

3. Pageants, Processions, and Feasts.—The following are samples of a great number of similar entries:—

1551. "The 2d daye of Nov. cam to London from Hamton Courtte and landyd at Benerd Castyll, the old Qwyne of Schottes" (this would be Mary, daughter of Claude de Lorraine, Duke of Guise, who married King James V. of Scotland in 1515, was mother of Mary Queen of Scots, and died in 1560), "and cam rydyng to the bysshope pallas at Powlles, with many lordes, the Duke of Suffolke, &c. . . . and then the Qwyne and alle her owne lades and her gentyll women was to the nombre of C (100), and ther was sent her mony grett gyftes by the Mayre and Aldermen as beyffes, mottuns, velles, swines, bred, wylld ffule, wynes, bere, spysys, and alle thinges, and qwaylles, sturgeon, wod and colles, and samons by dyvers men," and very useful "gyfftes" too, although the "qwaylles," if by that whales are meant, would be rather cumbrous presents to take away with her, but possibly they were quails.

"September 30th, 1552, the Mayre and the alderman and the new shreyffes took berges at III Cranes in the Vyntre, and so to Westmynstre Hall, and ther they tote hoyth (oath) in the excheker, and then they cam to dener. Ther was as grett a dener as youe have sene, for ther wher mony gentyll men and women."

In 1553 the new Lord Mayor went to Westminster, attended by "the craftes of London in ther best liveray, with trumpets blohyng and whets (waits) playing, . . . all the craftes barges with stremers and banars, and so to the cheker, and so homwards." They landed at "Banard Castyll," and arranged a procession in "Powlle's Chyrche yerde." . . . "Furst wher 2 tall men bayreng 2 great stremors of the

Marchand Tayllers' armes; then cam on (with a) drume and a flutt playing, and a nodur with a gret f——, and alle they in blue sylke; and then cam 2 gret wodyn (woodmen) with 2 gret clubes, alle in grene and with skwybes (squibs) bornyng, with gret berds and syd here (great beards and side hair), and 2 targetts upon their bakes . . . and then cam XVI. trumpetrs blohyng . . . and then a duyllyll (devil); and after cam the bachelors alle in a leveray and skarlett hods; and then cam Sant John Baptyst, gorgyusly, with goody speches . . . and then my Lord Mayre and 2 good henchmen, and then alle the althermen and shreyffes, and so to dener, and after dener to Powlle's, and alle them that bere tergetts dyd (bear) after stayff torchys with all the trumpets and wettes (waits) blowhyng, thrugh Powlles, round abow the quiers and the body of the chyrche blowhyng, and so home to my Lord Mere's howsse."

"July 2nd, 1555, was the Merchand Tayllers' fest, and ther dyned my Lord Mayre and dyvers of the counselle and juges, and the shreyffes, and mony althermen and gentyllmen, and they had agaynst ther dener 58 bokes (bucks) and two stages (stags)." A somewhat plentiful banquet, after which followed the appointment of the warden and other officers for the ensuing year. "Alle five borne in London, and tayller sounes alle."

"1556. The furst daye of September was Sant Gylles Day, and ther was a goodly procession abowt the parryche (St. Giles', Cripplegate), with the whettes (waits), and the canape borne and the sacrament, and ther was a goodly masse songe as bene herd (as has been heard), and Master Thomas Grenelln, waxchandler, mad a grett dener for Master Garter and my lade (lady), and Master Machylle the shereyff and ys wyff, and boyth the chamberlayns, and mony worshepefull men and women at dener, and the whettes playing and dyvers odur mynstrelles, for ther was a grett dener."

"10th June, 1560. Feast of the compane of Skyners and ther mony worshepefull men wher at dener, for ther was a worshepefull dener." After which is narrated the election of the master and other officers of the company for the coming year, "and Master Clareshur mad a grett bankett for the master and hys compene, furst spysed bred, cheres (cherries), straberes, pepyns, and marmalade and suckett comfets, and portingalles

(Portugal oranges), and dyvers odur dyssays, (dishes), epocres, rennys (Rhenish wine), claret wyne, and bere, and alle grett plente and alle was welcome." Not quite so substantial a repast as that of the Merchant Taylors with their 58 bucks and 2 stags.

4. Amusements.—Although the fires of Smithfield during the reign of Mary overcanopied the City with a cloud of gloom, and notwithstanding the people had a constant source of delectation in witnessing the hangings and quarterings, and ear-lopping on pillories, the whippings at cart-tails, and the penance-doing at Paul's Cross, of rogues and heretics, they found time to amuse themselves in other ways, sometimes perhaps in sports of a rough and barbarous character, at others of a simpler and unobjectionable nature, of which the favourite was dancing round the maypole, but always accompanied by loud and boisterous shouts of merriment. Machyn frequently refers to these pastimes. The following are specimens:—

"May 26th, 1552. Cam into Fa(nchurch) parryche a goodly maypole as you h(ave seen), pentyd whyt and gren, and ther the men and women dyd wher abowt ther neke baldrykes of whyt and gren : the gyant, the mores danse, and the —— had a castylle in the myd with pensels and a —— plasys of sylke and gilded, and the sam (day the) Lord Mayre by conselle causyd yt to be (taken) done and broken."

"December 9th, 1554. At afternon was a bere baytin on the Banksyde, and ther the grett blynd bere broke losse, and on runnyng away he chakt (caught) a servyng manne by the calff of the legge and bit a grett pease away, and after by the hokyl (ancle) bone, that within 3 days after he ded (died)."

"1557. May 30th was a goly (jolly) May-game in Fanchyrch Street, with drumes and gunes and pykes, and nine wordes (worthies) dyd ryd; and they had speches evere man, and the morris dansse, and the saudon (soldan or sultan) and a elevant (elephant) with a castyll and the sauden and young morens (Moors) with targettes and darttes, and the lord and lade of the Maye."

The sextons' merry-making was of a more sober kind as befitted their craft, thus: "1554. June 25th, anodur masse kept at the Gray freers for the saxtons of London and after pressessyon, with the whetes plahyng and clarkes syngyng thrug Chepesyd unto Soper Lane and again thrug

Powlles-chyrchyard, by master denes (house) and thrug Warwick Lane unto Gray freers, and so to dener unto the Kukes' (Cooks') hall."

5. Punishment.—"November 4th, 1554. Master Harpfield preched at Powlles Crosse, when ther wher fyve did penans with shetts (sheets) abowt them and tapurs and rods in ther handes, and the prycher dyd stryke them with a rod, and ther did they stand tyll the sermon was well done. On of these was a priest some tyme chanon at Eyssyng Spyttyll; three of them were relegyous men (monks or friars), and the fifth a temporall man that had two wyeffes."

"1559. The 20th August was Sonday: ther was a sarmon at Powlles Crosse; ys name was ———, and ther was a menester dyd penans for the marchyng of a setenn cupolle that was mared (married) afor tym."

"1551, May 2nd. The same day was hangd at Tyburne IX fellows. The same year on the 12th September there was hanged IX women and II men."

"1562, June 27th. Whent to Tyburne; V men and VI women for to hange for theft."

These were "the good old times" that poets rave about.

"1554. The XVII day of Septembre a proclamasyon that alle vacabonds and loitherus boyth Englysmen and alle maner of strangers that have no master should avoid the cete (City) and subarbes apon gret pain." An edict which appears to have been speedily put in force, as we read a day or two after :-

"Two men wher wyped about London after a carts hors for loythring, and as wagabones." Also, "A lad was wypd at the post in Chepe for ronnyng abowt masterless as a vagobond."

"August 19th, 1552. Ther was a mon in the (pillory) in Chepe for spykyng agaynst the Mayre and his br(ethren)."

"1559. Desembre 18th, did a woman ryd uponc (a horse) with a paper on her hed for boderie with a basen ryngyng."

1558-9, February 18th and 20th. "A man stood in the pelerc with a coler of smelts aboutt his neke for buying them as taken for the Qhwen" (by pre-emption) "and sold them at his vantage amonge the fyswyffes."

"November 29th, 1560. Ther was a man ryd for bryngyng messele (measly) porke to selle." A very wholesome punishment, which might be revived with advantage amongst some of our sausage dealers. It would appear that the French notion of John Bull selling his wife in Smithfield is not altogether without foundation, as we read: "The XXIII day of Novembre, 1553, dyd ryd in a cort cheken parsun of sant Necolas Cold Abby round abowt London, for he sold ys wyff to a bowcher."

"1561. June 25th. Two pelores in Chepsyd, wher wer sett seven men for kungaryng (conjuring)." It is fortunate for Messrs. Maskelyne and Cook that they live in the nineteenth and not in the sixteenth century.

"1555. XXIX April, a man bawd was putte in the pelore for bryngyng men's prentes (tradesmen's apprentices) harlots, the wyche they gayff hym and them serten of their masters' goodes and wasted." And richly did the rascal deserve the punishment; it is to be hoped he was well pelted with rotten eggs.

Ring-dropping appears not to be a modern dodge of roguery, but of the venerable age of three centuries at least, for we find that in 1553, April 17th, "a man was put in the pelere for fasshele (falsely) deseyvyng of the Qhwens subgettes, sellyng of ryngs for golde and was nodur seylver nor golde but cowper, the wyche he has deseyved money; thys was done in Chepe." Also on July 3rd in the same year, "A man was wypyd abowtt the post of reformacyon (a very good name) be the standard in Chepsyd for sellyng of false ryngs."

The year 1557 was a glorious one for householders, for on September 5th in that year " was a proclamasyon mad that the bochers of London shold selle beyffe and moton and velle, the best for a penny fordyng the pound, and nekes and legges at iii fordynges the pound, and the lambe the quorter viiid., and yff they wyll not thay loysse ther fredom for ever and ever."

The fire brigade of 1557 was on a very moderate scale as compared with that of the present year of grace, and the members had charitable and religious duties imposed on them which the brigade of modern times would scarcely consider as coming within the sphere of their duty. We read: " Jan. 7th, 1556-7, in Chosdwener Street Word a bellman was appointed to go round the ward and ring his bell at the strett ends in case of fire, and to helpe the powre (poor) and pray for the ded."

Index.

Abbey of St. Mary of Graces, 208; abbots of, 216
Aldgate, 22; churches, 181; attacked, 192; barons in, 190
Aldersgate Street, 118; Aldersgate, 24; churches, etc., 123
Amusements, 285
Anne of Bohemia, 55
Annesley, Samuel, 112
Artillery company, 93
Audley, Sir Thomas, 193

Bailly, Harry, 169
Bakers punished, 48
Bancroft, Francis, 108
Basset, Fulco, 262
Baynard's Castle, 232
Bishop, a brave old London, 262
Bishopgate, 26; in charge of Hanseatic merchants, 27
Bishopsgate Street, 76
Bowdicea, 3
Braybrooke, Robert de, Bishop of London, 249
Brember, Sir Nicholas, 236
Bridgegate, 31
British village, the, 2
Burning heretics, 276
Butchers' price of meat fixed, 290

Canterbury pilgrims, 170
Canute attacks London, 13
Charter, the Conqueror's, 220
Chaucer and the Tabard, 165
Churches, 35, 38, 43, 80, 81, 86, 87, 126, 127, 146, 181, 188, 195
Conduits, 37
Convent of St. Clare, 197
Cooks, 136
Cooper, Sir Astley, 145
Coronation, Queen Eleanor, 44
Cottage hospitals, 195
Cripplegate, 28
Cromwell family, 84-5
Crosses and images burnt, 277
Crosby, Sir John, 99
Crown Field, 36
Curfew, 36, 125

D'Albret, Sir Perducas, 241
Diarist, an old London, 269
Ditch, London, 30
Dowgate, 26
Drowning, execution by, 229
Dunmow flitch, 224

Edward III. in peril, 208-9, 236
Eleanor Cross, the, 38, 71
Excise Office, 150
Executions, 37; *re* Wyatt's rebellion, 274

Falcasius and the justice, 250
Fauconbridge, 23
Fires, incendiary, 138; bellman at, 290
Fitzwalter, Baron, of Baynard Castle, 219; service and privileges, 225-6
Foreign merchants, 27, 61-64
Funerals, 278

Gates, 5, 22
Glass, 149
Gloucester, Duke of, 241-4
Gresham, Sir Thomas, 104; Sir John, funeral, 280
Grocers' Company, 238

Helwood, Peter, 128
Henry III., 46
Henry VI., 56
Henry VIII., 57-60
Hoadley, Benjamin, 148
Holbein, Hans, 189
Holdsworth, Richard, 147
Hostelries, 136-8
Howard, Lord Edward, 65
Houses, historic, 99, 102-4, 106, 131-6, 143-6; religious, and chapels, 87, 110-11, 113-15, 130, 153
Howell, James, 150
Hurricane, A.D. 1091, 35

Iconoclasm, 276
Inns, 96
Inscription, curious, 10

INDEX.

James I. enters London, 139
Jews, usury, massacre, etc., 49, 50; synagogue, 115
Joscelyne, Ralph, re walls, 17

Katherine of Valois, 55
Knighten Guild, 185
Knollys, Hansard, 114
Knowles, Sir Robert, 241

Leathersellers' Company, 93; charters, 94; halls, 95
Lollards, 259
London, pillaged, 4; fortified, A.D. 1643, 19; Roman remains, 77
Longbeard, W. Fitzosbert, 42
Lord Mayor's Day, 66
Louis XIV., anecdote, 91
Lud, King, 25
Ludgate, 25
Lydgate, 39

Machyn, Henry, 269; diary, extracts from, 274
Marching watch, 56-60
Margaret of Anjou, pageant, 55
Matilda the Fair, 222-3
Matilda, Queen, 179
May Day, the Evil, 62
Mayors and aldermen, 122
Merchants' lecture, 156
Miracle plays, 257
Moorgate, 30

Nevil, Sir Thomas, 192
Newgate, 28; John Offrem's escape, 29
Norman, Prior, 183, 186
Norman, Sir John, 67

Old Bishopsgate, 116
Old Broad Street, 142; public buildings in, 161
Old Jewry, 48

Pageants, 55, 68, 281
Pamphlets, 73
Papey, the, 87
Paulet, Sir William, 144
Pawnbrokers, 195
Pestilence, 191
Pickaxe Street, 118
Pillory, 276-7

Pinder, Sir Paul, 101
Pinmakers, 152
Plantagenet, Edmund, 200
Post Office, 99
Praed, 97
'Prentices, 39
Printers and publishers, 140
Priory and Hospital of Bethlehem, 88
Priory and Hospital of the Holy Trinity, 178
Punishment, 287

Radcot Bridge, affair of, 246
Richard II., 237
Riots, goldsmiths' and tailors', 51
Roman Catholicism—Queen Mary —275
Roman remains, 77
Royal Society, the, 105

Seals, St. Helen's, 83; St. Mary of Graces, 217
Scott, John, D.D., 148
Sildham, 54
St. Augustine's, 153
St. Bartholomew, fracas at, 265
St. Clare, 199
St. Mary Spital, 86
St. Paul's, 256

Tabard, the, 166
Temple Bar, 32
Thames, Valley of the, 1
Tombs, St. Botolph, 81; St. Helen, 84
Tournament in Cheapside, 52
Traitors' quarters exposed, 122
Tresilian, Sir Robert, 245
Trinity Hall, 129
Tyler, Wat, slain, 240-1

Villeins, 212

Walls of London, 3-18
Walworth, Lord Mayor, 241
Wardhoke, 164
Wesley, John, 130
Wesleys, the, 112
Wife, sale of a, 289
William builds the Tower, 14
Workhouse founded, 107
Wyclif, 254

Elegantly bound in cloth gilt, demy 8vo., 6s.

Legendary Yorkshire.

By FREDERICK ROSS, F.R.H.S.

Contents:—The Enchanted Cave—The Doomed City—The Worm of Nunnington—The Devil's Arrows—The Giant Road Maker of Mulgrave—The Virgin's Head of Halifax—The Dead Arm of St. Oswald the King—The Translation of St. Hilda—A Miracle of St. John—The Beatified Sisters—The Dragon of Wantley—The Miracles and Ghost of Watton—The Murdered Hermit of Eskdale—The Calverley Ghost—The Bewitched House of Wakefield.

PRESS OPINIONS.

Beverley Recorder says—"It is a work of lasting interest, and cannot fail to delight the reader."

Driffield Observer says—"The history and the literature of our county are now receiving marked attention, and Mr. Andrews merits the support of the public for the production of this and the other interesting volumes he has issued. We cannot speak too highly of this volume, the printing, the paper, and the binding being faultless."

Elegantly bound in cloth gilt, demy 8vo., 6s.

Yorkshire ✠ Family ✠ Romance.

By FREDERICK ROSS, F.R.H.S.

Contents:—The Synod of Streoneshalh—The Doomed Heir of Osmotherley—St. Eadwine, the Royal Martyr—The Viceroy Siward—Phases in the Life of a Political Martyr—The Murderer's Bride—The Earldom of Wiltes—Blackfaced Clifford—The Shepherd Lord—The Felons of Ilkley—The Ingilby Boar's Head—The Eland Tragedy—The Plumpton Marriage—The Topcliffe Insurrection—Burning of Cottingham Castle—The Alum Workers—The Maiden of Marblehead—Rise of the House of Phipps—The Traitor Governor of Hull.

PRESS OPINIONS.

"The grasp and thoroughness of the writer is evident in every page, and the book forms a valuable addition to the literature of the North Country."—*Gentlewoman.*

"Many will welcome this work."—*Yorkshire Post.*

HULL: WILLIAM ANDREWS & CO., THE HULL PRESS.
London: Simpkin, Marshall, Hamilton, Kent, & Co., Ld.

Elegantly bound in cloth gilt, demy 8vo., price 6s.

Old Church Lore.

By WILLIAM ANDREWS, F.R.H.S.,

Author of "Curiosities of the Church," "Old-Time Punishments," "Historic Romance," etc.

CONTENTS.

The Right of Sanctuary—The Romance of Trial—A Fight between the Mayor of Hull and the Archbishop of York—Chapels on Bridges—Charter Horns—The Old English Sunday—The Easter Sepulchre—St. Paul's Cross—Cheapside Cross—The Biddenden Maids Charity—Plagues and Pestilences—A King Curing an Abbot of Indigestion—The Services and Customs of Royal Oak Day—Marrying in a White Sheet—Marrying under the Gallows—Kissing the Bride—Hot Ale at Weddings—Marrying Children—The Passing Bell—Concerning Coffins—The Curfew Bell—Curious Symbols of the Saints—Acrobats on Steeples—A carefully-prepared Index.

ILLUSTRATED

PRESS OPINIONS.

"A worthy work on a deeply interesting subject. . . . We commend this book strongly."—*European Mail.*

"An interesting volume."—*The Scotsman.*

"Contains much that will interest and instruct."—*Glasgow Herald.*

"The author has produced a book which is at once entertaining and valuable, and which is also entitled to unstinted praise on the ground of its admirable printing and binding."—*Shields Daily Gazette.*

"Mr. Andrews' book does not contain a dull page. . . . Deserves to meet with a very warm welcome."—*Yorkshire Post.*

"Mr. Andrews, in 'Old Church Lore,' makes the musty parchments and records he has consulted redolent with life and actuality, and has added to his works a most interesting volume, which, written in a light and easy narrative style, is anything but of the 'dry-as-dust' order. The book is handsomely got up, being both bound and printed in an artistic fashion."—*Northern Daily News.*

HULL: WILLIAM ANDREWS & CO., THE HULL PRESS.
London: Simpkin, Marshall, Hamilton, Kent, & Co., Ld.

SECOND EDITION.   Bound in cloth gilt, demy 8vo.   6s.

Curiosities of the Church:

Studies of Curious Customs, Services, and Records,

By WILLIAM ANDREWS, F.R.H.S.,

AUTHOR OF "HISTORIC ROMANCE," "FAMOUS FROSTS AND FROST FAIRS," "HISTORIC YORKSHIRE," ETC.

CONTENTS:

Early Religious Plays: being the Story of the English Stage in its Church Cradle Days—The Caistor Gad-Whip Manorial Service—Strange Serpent Stories—Church Ales—Rush-Bearing—Fish in Lent—Concerning Doles—Church Scrambling Charities—Briefs—Bells and Beacons for Travellers by Night—Hour Glasses in Churches—Chained Books in Churches—Funeral Effigies—Torchlight Burials—Simple Memorials of the Early Dead—The Romance of Parish Registers—Dog Whippers and Sluggard Wakers—Odd Items from Old Accounts—A carefully compiled Index.

ILLUSTRATED.

Press Opinions.

"A volume both entertaining and instructive, throwing much light on the manners and customs of bygone generations of Churchmen, and will be read to-day with much interest."—*Newberry House Magazine.*

"An extremely interesting volume."—*North British Daily Mail.*

"A work of lasting interest.—*Hull Examiner.*

"The reader will find much in this book to interest, instruct, and amuse."—*Home Chimes.*

"We feel sure that many will feel grateful to Mr. Andrews for having produced such an interesting book."—*The Antiquary.*

"A volume of great research and striking interest."—*The Bookbuyer (New York).*

"A valuable book."—*Literary World (Boston, U.S.A.).*

"An admirable book."—*Sheffield Independent.*

"An interesting, handsomely got up volume. . . . Mr. Andrews is always chatty and expert in making a paper on a dry subject exceedingly readable."—*Newcastle Courant.*

"Mr. William Andrews' new book, 'Curiosities of the Church,' adds another to the series by which he has done so much to popularise antiquarian studies. . . . The book, it should be added, has some quaint illustrations, and its rich matter is made available for reference by a full and carefully compiled index."—*Scotsman.*

HULL: WILLIAM ANDREWS & CO., THE HULL PRESS.
London: Simpkin, Marshall, Hamilton, Kent, & Co., Ld.

"Quite up to Date."—*Hull Daily Mail.*

Crown 8vo., 140 pp.; fancy cover, 1s.; cloth bound, 2s.

STEPPING-STONES TO SOCIALISM.

BY DAVID MAXWELL, C.E.

CONTENTS

In a reasonable and able manner Mr. Maxwell deals with the following topics:—The Popular Meaning of the Term Socialism—Lord Salisbury on Socialism—Why There is in Many Minds an Antipathy to Socialism—On Some Socialistic Views of Marriage—The Question of Private Property—The Old Political Economy is not the Way of Salvation—Who is My Neighbour?—Progress, and the Condition of the Labourer—Good and Bad Trade: Precarious Employment—All Popular Movements are Helping on Socialism—Modern Literature in Relation to Social Progress—Pruning the Old Theological Tree—The Churches,—Their Socialistic Tendencies—The Future of the Earth in Relation to Human Life—Socialism is Based on Natural Laws of Life—Humanity in the Future—Preludes to Socialism—Forecasts of the Ultimate Form of Society—A Pisgah-top View of the Promised Land.

PRESS OPINIONS.

The following are selected from a large number of favourable notices:—

"The author has evidently reflected deeply on the subject of Socialism, and his views are broad, equitable, and quite up to date. In a score or so of chapters he discusses Socialism from manifold points of view, and in its manifold aspects. Mr. Maxwell is not a fanatic; his book is not dull, and his style is not amateurish."—*Hull Daily Mail.*

"There is a good deal of charm about Mr. Maxwell's style."—*Northern Daily News.*

"The book is well worthy of perusal."—*Hull News.*

"The reader who desires more intimate acquaintance with a subject that is often under discussion at the present day, will derive much interest from a perusal of this little work. Whether it exactly expresses the views of the various socialists themselves is another matter, but inasmuch as these can seldom agree even among themselves, the objection is scarcely so serious as might otherwise be thought."—*Publishers' Circular.*

HULL: WILLIAM ANDREWS & CO., THE HULL PRESS.
London: Simpkin, Marshall, Hamilton, Kent, & Co., Ld.

www.ingramcontent.com/pod-product-compliance
Lightning Source LLC
Chambersburg PA
CBHW030748250426
43672CB00028B/1364